HANDBOOK of the National Catholic War Council

Published by Left of Brain Books

Copyright © 2021 Left of Brain Books

ISBN 978-1-396-32130-6

First Edition

All rights reserved. No part of this publication may be reproduced, distributed, or transmitted in any form or by any means, including photocopying, recording, or other electronic or mechanical methods, without the prior written permission of the publisher, except in the case of brief quotations embodied in critical reviews and certain other noncommercial uses permitted by copyright law. Left of Brain Books is a division of Left of Brain Onboarding Pty Ltd.

Table of Contents

PREFACE 1

CHAPTER I

1. PURPOSE OF THE NATIONAL CATHOLIC WAR COUNCIL 4

3. OPERATIVE COMMITTEES OF THE NATIONAL CATHOLIC WAR COUNCIL 9

    A. THE ADVISORY FINANCE COMMITTEE 9

    B. THE COMMITTEE ON SPECIAL WAR ACTIVITIES 10

        I. THE COMMITTEE ON FINANCE FOR SPECIAL WAR ACTIVITIES 12

        II. NATIONAL COMMITTEE ON WOMEN'S ACTIVITIES 12

        III. NATIONAL COMMITTEE ON MEN'S ACTIVITIES 16

        IV. THE NATIONAL CHAPLAINS' AID ASSOCIATION 18

        V. NATIONAL COMMITTEE ON CATHOLIC INTERESTS 22

        VI. NATIONAL COMMITTEE ON RECONSTRUCTION AND AFTER-WAR ACTIVITIES 22

        VII. NATIONAL COMMITTEE ON HISTORICAL RECORDS 23

    C. KNIGHTS OF COLUMBUS COMMITTEE ON WAR ACTIVITIES 25

4. THE PROBLEMS OF THE NATIONAL CATHOLIC WAR COUNCIL 29

CHAPTER II

THE CATHOLIC ARMY AND NAVY CHAPLAIN BUREAU 34

CHAPTER III

FORMATION OF DIOCESAN WAR COUNCILS 37

1. SUGGESTED PLANS FOR ORGANIZATION 37

2. COOPERATIVE COMMITTEES OF THE DIOCESAN WAR COUNCIL ... 40
3. NATIONAL AND DIOCESAN COOPERATION ... 46
4. COOPERATIVE WORK OF THE PARISHES ... 47

CHAPTER IV

GOVERNMENTAL AND SUPPLEMENTAL AGENCIES IN WAR WORK ... 51

1. NECESSITY OF COOPERATION ... 51
2. THE PRINCIPAL AGENCIES OF COOPERATION ... 52
   A. GOVERNMENTAL AGENCIES ... 52
      I. DEPARTMENT OF THE TREASURY ... 52
      II. DEPARTMENT OF WAR AND NAVY ... 57
      III. DEPARTMENT OF AGRICULTURE ... 60
      IV. DEPARTMENT OF LABOR ... 63
      V. COUNCIL OF NATIONAL DEFENSE ... 69
      VI. UNITED STATES FOOD ADMINISTRATION ... 71
      VII. UNITED STATES FUEL ADMINISTRATION ... 76
      VIII. COMMITTEE ON PUBLIC INFORMATION ... 79
      IX. THE FEDERAL BOARD FOR VOCATIONAL EDUCATION ... 80
      X. THE AMERICAN NATIONAL RED CROSS ... 82
   B. SUPPLEMENTAL AGENCIES FOR COOPERATIVE WAR WORK ... 87
      I. THE YOUNG MEN'S CHRISTIAN ASSOCIATION ... 87
      II. THE YOUNG WOMEN'S CHRISTIAN ASSOCIATION ... 88
      III. THE JEWISH WELFARE BOARD ... 89
      IV. THE NATIONAL BOARD FOR HISTORICAL SERVICE ... 91

V. THE TRAVELERS AID SOCIETY 92

VI. THE NATIONAL AMERICAN COMMITTEE OF THE POLISH VICTIMS' RELIEF FUND 94

VII. THE AMERICAN COMMITTEE FOR ARMENIAN AND SYRIAN RELIEF 95

VIII. THE GENERAL WAR-TIME COMMISSION OF THE FEDERAL COUNCIL OF THE CHURCHES OF CHRIST IN AMERICA 96

IX. THE BOY SCOUTS OF AMERICA 97

X. THE NATIONAL ORGANIZATION FOR PUBLIC HEALTH NURSING, WAR PROGRAM COMMITTEE 100

PREFACE

This Handbook is written primarily for the purpose of describing in brief outline the causes which brought the National Catholic War Council into being and the problems which face the Catholic Church of the United States during the present war.

To make the world safe for Democracy, to establish peace in the world upon the tested foundations of political liberty, to champion the rights of mankind—such, in the words of President Wilson, is the task to which the American people have dedicated their lives, their fortunes, and their sacred honor. To accomplish this, the American Republic has had to sacrifice a principle upon which its policies have almost always been based; that of "Splendid Isolation." The President has told us that the chief obstacle at the beginning of the war was to overcome this traditional aloofness in world affairs. "The world is no longer," he has said, "divided into little circles of interest. The world no longer consists of neighborhoods. The world is linked in a common life and interest such as humanity never saw before. .... What disturbs the life of the whole world is the concern of the whole world, and it is our duty to lend the full force of this nation, moral and physical, to a league of nations which shall see to it that nobody disturbs the peace of the world without submitting his case first to the opinion of mankind."

In the world today the strongest response to this new internationalism must come from the Church of the ages. The Catholic Church cannot remain an isolated factor in the nation. The Catholic Church possesses spiritual and moral resources which are at the command of the nation in every great crisis. The message to the nation to forget local boundaries and provincialism is a message likewise to the Catholic Church. Parochial, diocesan and provincial limits must be forgotten in the face of the greater tasks which burden our collective religious resources. Today, as never before, the Catholic Church in the United States has an opportunity for doing a nation-wide work. No one, honestly, doubts Catholic loyalty to the principles of the American nation. And from the Hierarchy to the clergy, from the clergy to the people the *government expects an impulse towards a perfect and efficient cooperation with all its agencies in carrying the war to success.*

This Handbook has been designed to assist in this cooperation. Its chapters have been so divided that the reader may easily find that particular section which refers to their service in war work.

I recommend it most heartily to the Hierarchy, to the clergy and to our faithful people as a form for their activity.

JAMES CARDINAL GIBBONS,
Archbishop of Baltimore.

CHAPTER I

ESTABLISHMENT OF THE NATIONAL CATHOLIC WAR COUNCIL. PURPOSE AND SCOPE OF ITS ACTIVITIES. MEMBERS OF THE NATIONAL CATHOLIC WAR COUNCIL. THE COMMITTEES

CHAPTER I

ESTABLISHMENT OF THE NATIONAL CATHOLIC WAR COUNCIL. PURPOSE AND SCOPE OF ITS ACTIVITIES. MEMBERS OF THE NATIONAL CATHOLIC WAR COUNCIL. THE COMMITTEES

1. PURPOSE OF THE NATIONAL CATHOLIC WAR COUNCIL

When the declaration of war was made by the United States against the German Empire every part of the organization of the Church immediately became solicitous to do its share in assisting the Government. Activities of all kinds were begun by Catholic men and women in various parts of the country, and individual as well as corporate cooperation with such movements as the Belgium Relief, the Red Cross, the Liberty Loan, and others became the watchword. Shortly after the declaration of war, the loyalty of the Catholic Hierarchy, of the clergy and people was pledged anew to the country, to its Government and to its supreme Executive in a letter to President Wilson, drawn up by the Archbishops of the United States at their annual meeting in April, 1917, at the Catholic University of America. The following is the complete text of this important document, which was presented to the President by Cardinal Gibbons:

Standing firmly upon our solid Catholic tradition and history from the very foundation of this nation, we reaffirm in this hour of stress and trial our most sacred and sincere loyalty and patriotism toward our country, our Government, and our flag. Moved to the very depths of our hearts by the stirring appeal of the President of the United States and by the action of our national Congress, we accept wholeheartedly and unreservedly the decree of that legislative authority proclaiming this country to be in a state of war. We have prayed that we might be spared the dire necessity of entering the conflict. But now that war has been declared, we bow in obedience to the summons to bear our part in it, with fidelity, with courage, and with the spirit of sacrifice, which as loyal citizens we are bound to manifest for the defense of the most sacred rights and the welfare of the whole nation. Acknowledging gladly the gratitude that we have always felt for the protection of our spiritual liberty and the freedom of our Catholic institutions under the flag, we pledge our devotion and our strength in the maintenance of our country's glorious leadership in those possessions and principles which have been America's proudest boast. Inspired neither by hate nor fear, but by the holy sentiments of truest patriotic fervor and zeal, we stand ready, we and all the flock committed to our keeping, to cooperate in every way possible with our President and our national Government, to the end that the great and holy cause of liberty may triumph, and that our beloved country may emerge from this hour of test stronger and nobler than ever. Our people now, as ever, will rise as one man to serve the nation. Our priests and consecrated women will once again, as in every former trial of our country, win by their bravery, their heroism, and their service, new admiration and approval. We are all true Americans, ready, as our age, our ability, and our condition permit, to do whatever is in us to do, for the preservation, the progress, and the triumph of our beloved country. May God direct and guide our President and our Government, that out of this trying crisis in our national life may at length come a closer union among all the citizens of America, and that an enduring and blessed peace may crown the sacrifices which war inevitably entails.

Catholics throughout the United States naturally rejoiced at the large number of their co-religionists in the Army and Navy. It was clearly evident that the percentage of Catholics in the service was proportionately higher than the number of Catholics in the country. This happy result was an index of the patriotism of the Catholic body and, when the Government asked that organized lay agencies should take their share in caring for the soldiers and sailors, the Catholic body was eager to assist in the well-being of all the men in the service. But with the vast number of Catholic Societies willing and anxious to offer their services and with the untold resources of the Catholic Church throughout the country, the situation presented many delicate and difficult problems.

That a National Catholic organization of some kind was necessary after the entrance of the United States into the war on April 6, 1917, soon became apparent; and in August, under the direction and by the authority of their Eminences James Cardinal Gibbons, of Baltimore, John Cardinal Farley, of New York, and William Cardinal O'Connell, of Boston, a general Convention of the Catholics of the country was called.

This Convention met at the Catholic University of America, Washington, D. C., on August 11 and 12. There were present official representatives, clerical and lay, from sixty-eight dioceses of the United States, representatives of twenty-seven national Catholic organizations, and also of the entire Catholic press. Its objects were as follows: to promote the spiritual and material welfare of the United States troops during the war wherever they may be, at home or abroad, and to study, coordinate, unify and put in operation all Catholic activities incidental to the war.

At this Convention three things were decided upon: First, that all Catholic war activities should be unified and coordinated for greater efficiency; secondly, that local boards should be established in the various dioceses; and thirdly, that the Knights of Columbus be recognized as the body representing the Church in the recreational welfare of the soldiers in the camps.

The Convention pledged the united power and combined resources of the entire Catholic body and of all Catholic organizations to assist the Government in every need and problem arising from the war. Its members held themselves in readiness to cooperate in this work under the leadership of the Hierarchy. They placed on record their hearty approbation of the admirable regulations made by our War and Navy Departments for the safeguarding of our camps, cantonments, naval and military establishments from the moral dangers incidental to camp life. Formal resolutions to this effect were passed by the Convention, and as a result of this Convention, representatives were appointed by the Archbishops of the country, and for some months they planned the work of organization. In November, the Archbishops of the United States constituted themselves the National Catholic War Council and appointed as their Administrative Committee four Bishops.

The first meeting of the Administrative Committee was held at the Catholic University of America, on January 16, 1918. In his letter of January 12, 1918, calling the Administrative Committee together,

Cardinal Gibbons defined the task ahead of the four Bishops, namely: To direct and control, with the aid of the American Hierarchy, all Catholic activities in the war.

2. ORGANIZATION OF THE NATIONAL CATHOLIC WAR COUNCIL

The definite scope of the activities of the National Catholic War Council was agreed upon at a meeting in January, 1918, and the following plan was adopted:

I. The **NATIONAL CATHOLIC WAR COUNCIL**, composed of the fourteen Archbishops:

HIS EMINENCE JAMES CARDINAL GIBBONS, *Archbishop of Baltimore.*

HIS EMINENCE JOHN CARDINAL FARLEY, *Archbishop of New York.*

HIS EMINENCE WILLIAM CARDINAL O'CONNELL, *Archbishop of Boston.*

MOST REV. JOHN IRELAND, *Archbishop of St. Paul.*
MOST REV. ALEXANDER CHRISTIE, *Archbishop of Oregon City.*
MOST REV. JOHN J. GLENNON, *Archbishop of St. Louis.*
MOST REV. SEBASTIAN G. MESSMER, *Archbishop of Milwaukee.*
MOST REV. HENRY MOELLER, *Archbishop of Cincinnati.*
MOST REV. JOHN B. PITAVAL, *Archbishop of Santa Fe.*
MOST REV. JAMES J. KEANE, *Archbishop of Dubuque.*
MOST REV. EDWARD J. HANNA, *Archbishop of San Francisco.*
MOST REV. GEORGE W. MUNDELEIN, *Archbishop of Chicago.*
MOST REV. JOHN W. SHAW, *Archbishop of New Orleans.*
MOST REV. DENNIS J. DOUGHERTY, *Archbishop of Philadelphia.*

II. The **ADMINISTRATIVE COMMITTEE**, composed of the four Bishops:

RT. REV. PETER J. MULDOON, D. D., *Chairman.*
RT. REV. J. B. SCHREMBS, D. D.
RT. REV. PATRICK J. HAYES, D. D.
RT. REV. WM. T. RUSSELL, D. D.

VERY REV. JOHN F. FENLON, D. D., S. S., Secretary.

III. The EXECUTIVE COMMITTEE, composed of the four Bishops, six members of the Knights of Columbus War Council, and six members at large. The Executive Committee is an Advisory Board, and meets regularly for the general discussion of all national Catholic war activities. The following are its members:

RT. REV. BISHOP MULDOON, D. D.
RT. REV. BISHOP SCHREMBS, D. D.
RT. REV. BISHOP HAYES, D. D.
RT. REV. BISHOP RUSSELL, D. D.
RT. REV. MSGR. H. T. DRUMGOOLE, D. D., LL. D.
RT. REV. MSGR. M. J. SPLAINE, D. D.
RT. REV. MSGR. EDW. A. KELLY, D. D.
REV. JOHN J. BURKE, C. S. P.
JOHN G. AGAR.
DANIEL J. CALLAHAN.
WILLIAM J. MULLIGAN.
CHARLES I. DENECHAUD.
JAMES A. FLAHERTY.
WILLIAM J. MCGINLEY.
JAMES J. MCGRAW.
JOSEPH C. PELLETIER.

IV. The GENERAL COMMITTEE, composed of two representatives, one clerical and one lay, from each Diocese, two representatives from each national Catholic society, two representatives of the Catholic Press Association, two representatives of the Federation of

Catholic Societies, and such other members-at-large as the Committee of Bishops may choose. The General Committee is a larger advisory board which meets at the call of the Chairman of the Administrative Committee of Bishops whenever a general survey of national questions is to be made. On account of its size, difficulty and expense of travel, such a meeting is necessarily infrequent—perhaps once a year or on the occasion when a nation-wide Catholic financial drive is projected.

3. OPERATIVE COMMITTEES OF THE NATIONAL CATHOLIC WAR COUNCIL

The National Catholic War Council operates with regard to immediate war work on war problems through three principal committees, which are: The Advisory Finance Committee, the Committee on Special War Activities, and the Knights of Columbus Committee on War Activities.

A. THE ADVISORY FINANCE COMMITTEE

This Committee has the important duty of raising the national budget for Catholic War Activities of all kinds.

As an example of what one Catholic community can accomplish in efforts to raise funds for war activities, one of the most surprising and at the same time one of the most successful examples is that of the recent New York Catholic War Drive. In the Archdiocese over four and a half million dollars were raised.

The New York campaign was, in the widest and fullest sense of the term, a Catholic movement. The campaign was not conducted by any single organization; the aim from the beginning was to make the entire Catholic community, priests and laity, without exception of any individual or any organization of men and women, realize that it was their work and their responsibility. It is not too much to say that never in the history of the Church was the Catholic spirit of generosity and cooperation with the Government roused to such practical enthusiasm. Catholics realized, as never before, the strength of their Church, and they saw more clearly than ever the meaning and the value of Catholic unity. Not only did Catholics contribute but hundreds and thousands of Protestants and Jews gave generously, for prejudice had been broken down and a better understanding had arisen between all the citizens of the State. The success of this effort is a sure index of what can be expected in other parts of the country.

The following prominent Catholic citizens have been appointed by the Archbishops as members of the Advisory Finance Committee: Baltimore, James R. Wheeler; Boston, James J. Phelan; Chicago, John V. T. Murphy; Cincinnati, Charles Williams; Dubuque, J. J. Meyers; Milwaukee, Frank G. Smith; New Mexico, O. N. Marron; New Orleans, Charles Theard; New York, Adrian Iselin, Jr.; Philadelphia, I. J. Dohan; Portland, T. E. Sullivan; San Francisco, Edward J. Tobin; St. Louis, Festus J. Wade; St. Paul, Wm. P. Kenny.

B. THE COMMITTEE ON SPECIAL WAR ACTIVITIES

The Committee on Special War Activities, the Chairman of which is the Rev. John J. Burke, C. S. P., Editor of the *Catholic World*, and the Executive Secretary of which is Mr. Walter G. Hooke, of New York City, directs the work of the Standing Committees. These Committees are seven in number: Committee on Finance, Committee on Women's Activities, Committee on Men's Activities, Committee on Chaplains' Aid and Literature, Committee on Catholic Interests, Committee on Reconstruction and After-War Activities, Committee on Historical Records of Catholic War Activities.

The Seven National Standing Committees of the Committee on Special War Activities have offices at 930—32 Fourteenth Street, N. W., Washington, D. C. The different Chairmen and Secretaries are in constant attendance. Weekly staff meetings of the Committees are held and monthly meetings of the Committee on Special War Activities, the Rev. John J. Burke, C. S. P., presiding, are also held. The National Standing Committees give a monthly report on the progress of their activities to the

Committee on Special War Activities. Briefly the work outlined for these Committees may be described as follows:

I. THE COMMITTEE ON FINANCE FOR SPECIAL WAR ACTIVITIES
Chairman, MR. JOHN G. AGAR, NEW YORK

This Committee arranges the annual budget for the Committee on Special War Activities. Its duty is to supervise the payment of all appropriations made by the Committee and to care for all its financial accounts.

II. NATIONAL COMMITTEE ON WOMEN'S ACTIVITIES
Chairman, REV. WM. J. KERBY, PH.D.
Secretary, REV. JOHN COOPER, PH.D.

The war cannot be fought successfully without the help of the women of the country. There are innumerable tasks which women alone can perform. The opportunities which have arisen for the women in America are among the most wonderful in the history of the world.

The women of the country are actual sharers in the war. From their number must come nurses, accountants, aids in the hospitals, aids in the camps, and aids to travelers. One of the principal works of the Committee is the construction and supervision of Visitors' Houses, and this work commands the services of many organizations throughout the country. It is one of the most important fields of women's work in the service of their country.

Women are taking in this great war a part which, for diversity of work and intensity of effort is not in any way second to the part taken by the men. It was a foregone conclusion that our Catholic women would be as much interested and as eager to do their share of these various works as their sisters of other religious belief. Hence, the National Catholic War Council at its inception, turned its attention to the efforts of Catholic women and formed a Women's Committee for the general purpose of assisting the Catholic women of the country to utilize their efforts and energies in the most effective way to help win the war.

Before the Committee could be of any assistance to the women workers of the country, it was necessary to find out what the Catholic women were doing in the various phases of war work. Most of them were acting through their clubs, sodalities and societies, local or national. The first step in the carrying out of the Committee's purpose was to get in touch with these different organizations of Catholic women. If the Committee was to be helpful, it needed definite information as to what our resources in the way of women's societies were, what work they had accomplished, and what plans they had in mind. This task was entered upon by the Committee and is still in progress. A complete directory of all Catholic women's societies is being compiled. Through this directory, an accurate survey may be made of the work done. The tremendous energies of which our Catholic women are capable, may be coordinated to the best advantage, and loss, due to scattered effort and duplication, may be prevented. Where little or no war work has been accomplished, it is aimed to stimulate or create War Relief activities. Several thousands of these societies have already been registered and each day sees new ones added to the directory. The Committee asks that the presidents or secretaries of women's organizations send their names in to the National Committee so that the list may be complete.

As soon as they can be organized, Diocesan Committees on Women's Activities will be established in every diocese of the country. These units, being made up of the various societies of the diocese, will thus be brought into closer union and their work more carefully planned and more effectively carried out.

The National Women's Committee does not interfere in any way with individual organizations. The diocesan group will be the principal agency for the direction and strengthening of war activities in each particular diocese.

The function of the Women's National Committee is to obtain accurate information as to what our women are doing in the war, to know something of their resources and what they are capable of doing, to offer suggestions from time to time as to other works which may be done, continuance and increase of present work, and to submit a program of war relief measures which will be based on work actually done by Catholic women's organizations. It will be in a position also to know directly the needs of the Government and of our soldiers and sailors and to serve as a central agency of communication between the Government and the various bodies of Catholic women throughout the country. In a word, it hopes to supply our women with a channel for the more effective prosecution of war work and other national service.

Splendid work has already been done by the Catholic women of the United States. Yet much remains to be done. Each day that the war continues sees an increase of the possibilities for women's activities. Our Catholic women are capable, as experience has shown, of accomplishing truly great things, and it is the duty of the National Committee on Women's Organizations to coordinate all these activities.

The National Committee on Women's Activities desires the name and address of every organization and group of Catholic women in the United States, with a statement of the history and the address of each organization. It desires a list of the war activities already undertaken, either of a strictly Catholic nature or in cooperation with other organizations, either Catholic or non-Catholic. It seeks an indication of how much work has been done in the matter of knitting, sewing, collecting books for camp libraries, supplying religious articles and raising funds; and also a detailed account of all work undertaken for the protection of young girls. It asks suggestions upon the kind of work the organization is best prepared to do, and it asks also for information upon what is most needed to promote the Catholic women's war work in each community. It has been found particularly in those communities where troops are camping, when passing through, that clubs or rest rooms under proper Catholic auspices fill a most pressing need.

The National Committee offers the following suggested methods and types of war relief for Catholic women:

A. *General Recommendations.*

I. Intimate and cordial cooperation with governmental and non religious forces should be maintained. War service is thereby more wisely directed and effectively administered. For example:

    a. American Red Cross.
    b. Women's Committee, Council of National Defense.
    c. Food Administration.
    d. Fuel Administration.
    e. Local civic war agencies.
    f. Liberty Loans.

II. It will be found of real advantage to secure representation on local civic committees, thereby affording a wider application of Catholic principles and problems arising out of war relief.

B. *Social Work.*

I. Interest and care in the protection of young girls, through supervision of social conditions at camps and cantonments, and centers of war work.

II. Cooperation with Travelers' Aid Society or the establishment of equivalent relief where the Travelers' Aid Society is not in charge.

III. The proper housing of girls employed in war work, a need that has manifested itself where governmental service is being performed.

IV. Formation and development of girls' clubs.

V. To keep Catholic girls informed of government needs for women employees.

C. *Child Welfare Work.*
Care of children made dependent by the war. Maintenance of social activities impaired or threatened by war conditions.

D. *Canteen Service.*

E. *Educational.*

Lectures. Instructions on the causes of the war. Needs of the Government. Methods by which women can assist in war work.

Americanization of foreign-born. Teaching of English and civics. Speaking before foreign audiences.

Training of speakers for war topics, such as Liberty Loans, Food Conservation, etc.

Lectures on Home Economics.

F. *Recreational.*

Providing entertainment at the camps and cantonments. Visiting military hospitals, providing soldiers with fruit and delicacies, reading matter, arranging automobile tours of the city. Interest in and service in Visitors' Houses established at the various embarkation points and cantonments.

Providing proper amusement and methods of relaxation for the girl war workers.

G. *Religious Work.*

The making or providing funds for chaplains' outfits, providing rosaries, scapulars, medals, crucifixes for the soldiers.

III. NATIONAL COMMITTEE ON MEN'S ACTIVITIES
Chairman, MR. CHARLES I. DENECHAUD, New Orleans
Secretary, MR. MICHAEL JOHN SLATTERY, Philadelphia

At the outset of the war, one immediate duty presented itself: that of uniting the country into organizations for the purpose of rousing the spirit of the people in order that sick and wounded soldiers and families left destitute by absence or death of their wage-earners might not lack the care they needed. It is not sufficient for every man, woman and child in the country to give individual support to these national activities, such as the Red Cross, etc., for men and women of particular callings in life, of particular creeds, or of particular capacity should unite in order that such cooperation be made more effective and lasting. The great patriotic societies of the country should be given this organized cooperation; everybody can increase his power of helping by joining with his neighbors for the common cause. We are living in an era of such organization. The world is carried along by it. As the parish is linked to the diocese by organization, so must the diocese be linked to the nation. The National Catholic War Council is the channel into which diocesan and parochial activities should flow. Every diocese has a host of agencies fully equipped to do all sorts of good work, and it is simply a question of harnessing these agencies under proper direction to obtain the desired results. Their effectiveness depends largely upon two things: First, the existence of a fairly definite, intelligent, and comprehensive program, steadily pursued, and second, harmony in actual work as well as in the planning. National efficiency demands an immediate toning up all the individual and institutional efficiency. It too must make sure that duplication of effort, waste and inefficiency are avoided. Prevention must be emphasized as the most efficient approach to war problems. Above all, there must be a plan for the mobilization of all of our diocesan resources to meet the intensified needs. The functions of the National Committee on Men's Activities are:

I. To ascertain from all possible sources what the immediate needs are, what is being done to meet them, by whom and how; what needs to be done; whether there are existing institutions and agencies to do the work; if not, what can and should be done to supplement their efforts.

II. To ascertain what welfare work is being done elsewhere, both in this country and abroad under war conditions, by what methods and with what results.

III. To record and classify all information obtained and place it at the disposal of those specially interested.

IV. To work for the unification and centralization of effort in meeting national and diocesan needs during war time.

V. To be a clearing house for all diocesan activities and to correlate the agencies of the American Red Cross, the Council of National Defense, the Army and Navy Commission on Training Camp Activities, etc.

VI. To secure the enlistment of volunteers, and to place these volunteers where their services will be most needed to carry on the work.

VII. To act in a advisory capacity to help to a wise solution of emergency problems as they arise.

VIII. An honest effort to cooperate in every way possible with other institutions and agencies at work solving war problems.

IX. The indication of ways in which this Committee can be of help, aid requests to it for counsel and assistance where-ever needed.

The National Committee will give the Diocesan War Committee on Men's Activities:

a. Continued information as to what this Committee is doing and planning to do, especially as touching its field.

b. Prompt information of all facts coming to the Committee's attention, knowledge of which it is believed will prove helpful.

c. Notification of any special emergency which might arise demanding prompt attention.

d. Information from time to time as to what is being done elsewhere in the country and abroad, in its line.

e. Constructive suggestions from time to time.

The National Committee also desires a record of the number of men enlisted in the service and requests information and suggestions as to how best to promote Catholic men's war work in the community. It requires also from each organization a close cooperation with the Committee on Historical Records by sending clippings from local newspapers, photographs and other material concerning the activities of the organization in the war.

IV. THE NATIONAL CHAPLAINS' AID ASSOCIATION

The Chaplains' Aid Association is under the direction of the Committee on Special War Activities, of the National Catholic War Council, Washington, D. C. Its report is made regularly to the Administrative Committee of Bishops. Throughout the country it has established various Chapters. The first Chapter to be established was that of New York, and this particular Chapter has, because it is at a shipping point and port where almost all the troops leave for Europe, been made the central distributing office, where all reports are correlated and published in the *Bulletin*. Each Chapter has the right to have its own regulations, to collect and distribute its own funds, etc. Details of organization may be obtained by writing to 932 Fourteenth street, N. W., Washington, D. C., or 605 Fifth Avenue, New York. For the sake of economy, unity of action, etc., all Chapters are requested to keep in touch with the National Headquarters in Washington.

Chapters may be formed in any diocese with the approval of the Bishop. The Chaplains' Aid is now more than a year old, during which time the following Chapters have been formed:

Boston	Pittsfield, Mass.	Newark
Trenton	New Orleans	Wheeling
Philadelphia	Pittsburgh	Sharon, Pa.
Pottsville. Pa.	Norfolk, Va.	Canton, Ohio
Chatanooga	Jacksonville	Odell, Ill.
Cincinnati	Massillon, Ohio	Cascade, Iowa
Indianapolis	Burlington, Wis.	Buffalo
Morris, Minn.	Rome, N. Y.	Syracuse
Utica (two)	Rochester (two)	Whitesboro

During the same time, all the Chaplains of Army and Navy, and our troops both at home and abroad have been and are being furnished with Chaplains' outfits, religious articles, literature and other needful supplies.

The spiritual welfare of the soldier and sailor is the special field of the Chaplains' Aid. It would be impossible here to review everything that has been done. But it may be noted that through the various Chapters of the Chaplains' Aid, Chaplains' outfits, or kits as they are popularly called, have been given to 550 Chaplains, commissioned or volunteer.

The large kit is for home service; the smaller, or trench kit, for foreign service. The latter, containing everything necessary for the celebration of Mass, weighs, with case, 22 pounds.

The Chaplains' Aid has published, with a special introduction by Cardinal Gibbons, the Army and Navy Testament. Special plates had to be made. The first edition was of 10,000 copies; the second edition, of 50,000 copies; and the third edition, now ready, is of 500,000 copies. Of these, 200,000 copies have been distributed.

Following are the figures of some supplies sent out to the Chaplains:

Prayer-books (including those in Polish, Slovak and Italian)	340,000
Rosaries	121,000
Scapulars	196,000
Scapular medals	67,000
Catechisms (including Italian)	22,000
Hymn books and hymn cards	17,000
Sacred Heart badges	17,000
Pamphlets and tracts	176,000
Crucifixes	7,000
Religious Books	4,000

The number of linens supplied to Chaplains, including many sets beyond those placed in the kits, makes a total of 10,500.

About 500 sets of vestments have been supplied; also ciboria, monstrances, copes, missals and missal-stands, chalices, and other odd supplies to Chaplains, including altar wine, sanctuary oil, palms, incense and charcoal, portable organs, etc., etc.

A department of the Association is devoted to the furnishing of altar breads, weekly or bi-monthly, to Chaplains in the Army and Navy. Over 300,000 breads have been sent out.

Another department of the Chaplains' Aid Association provides magazines, books and all sorts of reading matter to camps and base hospitals, knitted afghans, games and puzzles and scrap-books. Comfort kits were provided at Christmas to the number of 1,500. The Red Cross received another consignment of 7,000, of which it was said, that it was the largest single contribution ever received by it.

The record of the work of the Association is preserved by means of a monthly *Bulletin*, of which twelve numbers have been published. This is sent out to Chaplains, to members and patrons, and to the various Chapters of the Association.

V. NATIONAL COMMITTEE ON CATHOLIC INTERESTS

Chairman, RT. REV. MONSIGNOR EDWARD A. KELLY, LL. D., Chicago.
Secretary, WALTER G. HOOKE, Washington, D. C.

The National Committee on Catholic Interests is chiefly concerned with watching the ruling of the various departments, with the view to bring sympathetically to various governmental agencies the Catholic position and sensibilities on questions of policy affecting the entire country. This Committee also serves as a medium of communication and exchange between the great national organizations in reaching Catholics and enlisting their cooperation in War Work. The membership of this Committee is large and contemplates prominent clergy and laymen in every diocese.

VI. NATIONAL COMMITTEE ON RECONSTRUCTION AND AFTER-WAR ACTIVITIES

Chairman, RT. REV. MONSIGNOR M. J. SPLAINE, D. D., Boston

If it is true that in time of Peace we should prepare for War, it is equally certain that in time of War we should prepare for Peace. Just as new and urgent problems arose upon the declaration of War, so upon the declaration of Peace will there arise gigantic problems of Reconstruction and After-War Activities which must not find us unprepared.

As a special committee of the National Catholic War Council in charge of this work, it is necessary that we devote our time and study in anticipating what those problems will be and in preparing as far as possible to be ready to meet them with proper remedies and solutions. We are interested in this work as Catholics because we are convinced that there is a distinct Catholic viewpoint to the work of Reconstruction and After-War Activities which is necessary in order to give the proper guarantee of moral correctness and beneficial results to the country as a whole.

It is now generally agreed that the colossal world war was brought about as the logical result of the practice of false philosophy and pernicious ethics. We must not go back to the old paths which lead to destruction, but we must endeavor as far as possible to base the principles that will hold the thought and action of the after-war era upon the Commandments of Almighty God and the teachings of Jesus Christ. For this purpose, a Committee of Catholic gentlemen who are careful students of the moral aspects of sociology, has been formed to devote its time and attention to studying the various problems that it is felt will arise, to begin to prepare the public mind by writing and publishing the teachings of the Catholic Church in regard to the true social welfare of mankind. It is hoped that as our great armies will be demobilized and will be reabsorbed into the industrial life of the nation, they will be able to return to conditions that will have been purified and corrected, because they will have been founded upon the Eternal principles of religion and morality which the Catholic Church has been commissioned by Almighty God to teach to the world in all places and at all times unto its consummation.

VII. NATIONAL COMMITTEE ON HISTORICAL RECORDS

Chairman, RT. REV. MONSIGNOR HENRY T. DRUMGOOLE, LL. D., Philadelphia.

Secretary, REV. PETER GUILDAY, PH.D., Washington, D. C.

The Committee on National Catholic War Records has been directed by the Administrative Committee of Bishops to bend every effort to secure immediately, and to preserve, an accurate and complete record of all Catholic American activity in the present war. This part of the National Catholic War Council cannot be too strongly emphasized. Unless we make provision for the history of Catholic patriotism and effort in this war, we shall be guilty of neglect which can never be remedied and of a mistake which can never be retrieved. If we fail to establish authentic records of our civic and religious activities, if we fail to record all noble impulses that enrich the hearts of American Catholics, we rob the Church of the future of inspiration, example and interpretation. History cannot be written on the day on which it is made, but preparations for that future history are all-important. The creation of archives, the careful preservation of every record and document, the description of every kind of spiritual and patriotic service, must be counted along the elementary duties of Catholic life today. The procuring of such a record will require the general assistance of all Catholics, especially the sympathetic cooperation of every Bishop and priest, particularly of every pastor, of the heads of Catholic societies of men and women, and of the Catholic press. Every Catholic should make his contribution to the history of the Church's activity in the war. The National Catholic War Council has felt the thrill of many great impulses, and has had the vision of many great impulses, but no one means more in the summing up than that of leaving to posterity accounts of Catholic aspiration and sacrifice in these troubled days. The Committee on Historical Records is endeavoring to do for Catholic activities what the National Board for Historical Service is accomplishing for the nation at large. Under the guidance of twenty of the foremost historical students of the country, the National Board for Historical Service has as its objects to facilitate the coordination and development of historical activity in the United States, to aid in supplying the general public with trustworthy information of historical or similar character, and to aid, encourage and organize agencies in different cities and localities for the purpose of preserving the record of war activities in these sections.

The Committee on Historical Records for the National Catholic War Council has divided this work into two main parts: First, the gathering of the census of the Catholic men and women in the service of the United States; second, the creation of national Catholic archives, where all materials relating to the aspect of Catholic activities in the war will be preserved and kept for future historians. The Committee desires, therefore, to secure at once for this census of Catholic men and women in the service the name, age, home address, branch of service, name and address of nearest relative or friend;

a. Of every Catholic man in the Army, Navy or Marines of the United States.
b. Of those examined and passed, even though not yet called to service.

    c. Of those serving in medical, hospital or ambulance corps;
    d. Of Chaplains, regular, non-commissioned, or auxiliary;
    e. Of helpers in cantonment, camp or overseas;
    f. Of every Catholic woman serving as nurse or in other governmental capacity.

Further information and material desired for the national Catholic archives may be broadly defined as follows:

Episcopal pronouncements, acts, addresses, books, pamphlets; likewise those of priests; church celebrations, prayers; congregational celebrations, activities; group or individual participation on the part of either clergy or laity.

Every bit of help in compiling the National Catholic War Records will count for the honor of Church and country, and for the glory of the men who are offering their life's blood, and of the women, who, in their husbands, sons and brothers, are giving of their heart's blood for God and the Right.

C. KNIGHTS OF COLUMBUS COMMITTEE ON WAR ACTIVITIES

Chairman, MR. WM. J. MULLIGAN, 461 Fourth Avenue, New York City.

Vice-Chairman, MR. DANIEL J. CALLAHAN, Norfolk & Washington Steamboat Company, Washington, D. C.

Secretary, MR. WM. J. MCGINLEY, New Haven, Conn.

MR. JAMES A. FLAHERTY, New Haven, Conn.

MR. JOSEPH C. PELLETIER, Barristers Hall, Boston, Mass.

MR. JAMES J. MCGRAW, Ponca City, Oklahoma.

MR. WM. P. LARKIN, 461 Fourth Avenue, New York City.

Washington Office, Woodward Building, Washington, D. C., is in charge of the Vice-Chairman and keeps in touch with the Government Departments.

New Haven Office is in charge of the Secretary and is the main office of the Committee. This office handles the entire domestic service.

New York Office, in charge of Mr. Wm. P. Larkin, handles matters in connection with the foreign service.

When the United States troops were being assembled along the Mexican Border in 1916, the Knights of Columbus, answering a number of appeals, ventured into a new field of work, namely, the establishment and conduct of buildings as recreation centers for the men in the service.

The buildings were erected at fifteen different points, thereby furnishing the soldiers, regardless of creed, with recreation and amusement, at the same time paying a special attention to the religious needs of the Catholics.

All this was done without any appeal to the public for funds, or any call upon its members. The cost was entirely defrayed out of the General Fund of the Order, or by dint of much economy in many other directions.

In addition to the work above indicated, local councils of the Order located adjacent to the camps furnished entertainment and social advantages to the soldiers visiting their locality on leave or furlough.

This work received the commendation of the War Department, of officers, privates and the public generally.

Upon the declaration of war on April 6, 1917, by President Wilson, the appeals again commenced for us to take up similar work at the camps, cantonments, encampments, naval bases and allied centers, with the result that we tendered our services, which were accepted by the Secretary of War and Committee on War Activities in June, 1917, and later by the Secretary of the Navy.

A letter from Secretary of War Baker dated September 23, 1917, gives briefly our status and his view:

"The Young Men's Christian Association represents the Protestant denomination, which will constitute roughly 60 per cent of our new Army; the work of this organization in all military camps both in Canada and abroad is too well known to require comment. The Knights of Columbus represent the Catholic denomination, which will constitute perhaps 35 per cent of the new Army. While this society is a fraternal organization, it will sustain exactly the same relation to the camps as is sustained by the Young Men's Christian Association and will hold no meetings to which all the troops in the camp are not invited regardless of religious or other preferences."

Our work consisted in the organization and maintenance of one or more buildings at each of the many centers of military activity. "Everything free, everybody welcome," was the slogan. Small libraries were established, free writing material, pianos, victrolas, moving picture machines, checkers, dominoes, pool and billiards, boxing outfits, basket-ball paraphernalia, base-ball outfits are some of the many diversions offered to the men. In addition, concerts, theatricals, vaudeville, lectures etc., are given frequently and always without charge. The buildings have been freely used by the Government for classes in athletics, lecturing on war tactics, etc.

To Jews has in many places been given free use of buildings for their services.

Priests selected by the ecclesiastical authorities, and later by Right Reverend Bishop Hayes of New York, have been supported by the Order, as and when appointed to various places here and overseas.

Financial assistance has been given to local councils adjacent to the camps upon request, to help them in their service work.

Overseas the work has been similar, although it was not until December 1, 1917, that we obtained the necessary permission from General Pershing to do this work. Our overseas Commissioner then returned to this country to discuss the matter of organization, etc., returning to France the middle of March, so that our overseas work practically commenced only on that date. Before his return, however, at the end of December, he had placed twenty volunteer Knights of Columbus Chaplains, sent abroad at our expense, but up to December 1, 1917, unable to enter upon the work until General Pershing had given the required permission. He also left money with the Chaplains and with many of the regular Army Chaplains to be expended for the welfare of the men, pending the starting of our organization upon his return.

In Boston a Service House with forty free beds has been opened, and another with 300 is being prepared. New York, Detroit and other cities are entering into this city service work on a large scale—all in addition to the work above referred to as being done by councils adjacent to the camps.

The work overseas, while aiming at the same ends, must necessarily be accomplished in a somewhat different way from that in this country. The really great service must be at the front, in and just behind the trenches. Here spiritual comforts and creature comforts are most needed, and yet the kind of war the change of scene, the movements of our men are such that buildings of anything like a permanent form are not advisable, while at the ports of entry and large naval bases, permanent buildings can be erected and conducted.

We are sending abroad automobiles, auto-trucks, auto-kitchens, all sorts of games, tobacco, cigarettes, chocolate, candy, soup cubes, etc.

Up to date no canteen has been established, and it is hoped that whatever we have may be given free as far as it will go.

No women, except a few in Paris, have been engaged for our work, either here or overseas. Our present policy is to supply only men who under the designation of secretaries, seem able to furnish all the service needed for the men.

Summary

150 buildings in eighty-three military, naval or allied centers in the United States.

350 secretaries in the United States.

75 Volunteer Knights of Columbus chaplains in the United States.

150 additional buildings planned for.

75 buildings in sixty places in France.

35 volunteer Knights of Columbus Chaplains in France, and arrangements being made for use of a considerable number of English-speaking French priests assigned by the French Government to the American Forces.

200 Secretaries in France.

25 chaplains with money for men's welfare.

200 additional buildings planned for.

The Knights of Columbus began their operations through a Central Bureau located in the Woodward Building, Washington D. C., but for reasons of more thorough efficiency and of prompter communication with its supreme directors, it was decided to move their administrative offices to the headquarters of the society at New Haven, Conn.

4. THE PROBLEMS OF THE NATIONAL CATHOLIC WAR COUNCIL

The main purpose of the National Catholic War Council is to give direction to the activity of the Catholic forces of the nation, in such a way that they may cooperate with the Government to their fullest extent in winning the present war. The National Catholic War Council was created to serve as best it might this coordination of Catholic activities, to afford means for a systematic study of national problems and to offer a national cooperation to the civic, social and moral agencies of the Church in the present emergency.

The old-time adjustments of our national life have been changed by the war. The pathways along which our energies have gone in the past have had to be recharted; and this recharting has not been accomplished without much confusion, many mistakes and long delays. But the determination to carry out this change has been unconquerable. The Federal Government and every State Government in the nation have rearranged all such relations.

The traditions of our history have been overthrown. Institutions have been modified. The purposes of peaceful life, which have given variety and manifold culture to our civilization, have been suspended on account of the war. Emergency has become our law, the rule of the nations' action, the key to its present spirit, and the measure of its supreme standards. University, high school, grammar school, factory, club, social organization, legislature and leadership, have all been brought into new relationship, each expressing in its own way a fraction of the integral life of the nation, whose forces are now assembled in one mighty effort to win the war.

Standards and purposes have been surrendered by all of these, and the new life of a nation is exacting a reorganization and a readjustment.

The splendor and majesty of the nation's ideals and the depth of its appeal to everything noble within us when its dignity is insulted and its sanctities profaned by the degrading touch of monstrous oppression are now shown forth as never before. National unity of a positive and directly active kind was only an aspiration before our entrance into the war; today it is the far-reaching and heart-searching policy of every patriot in the land, and the country's interests are the object of universal solicitude and unceasing prayer.

In the reconstruction necessary for the proper adjustment of Catholic activities to the state of war now existing, parochial ministrations, diocesan government, care of the moral and spiritual interests of our Catholic millions, cannot be lost sight of. The orderly procedure of the Church's work of sanctification must continue; but over and above these tasks have arisen new duties of sacrifice and new appeals for self-forgetting service. The problems which the Catholic Church in the United States face in this conflict are in many ways greater than many of the problems of the past. Where the soldier and the sailor go, the Church must send her chaplains to follow. The Church must face consciously the overwhelming problems of morality and spiritual reinforcement in the camp, in the community and on the battle line. It must foresee and guard against every new disguise of temptation that presents itself to the young of both sexes everywhere.

Millions of Catholics wish to do their duty nobly. They ask for direction, for opportunity to serve, for simplification of the problems of service. They are conscious of a two-fold purpose. One is to do their duty which love of country imposes; the other is to obey the fellowship of faith which brings within the realm of the supernatural motive every patriotic service to be undertaken.

The symbols of prayer and devotion which enrich our Catholic life and typify the sweet intimacy of our daily piety must be distributed among sailors and soldiers, with a care that knows no neglect. The material, mental and social needs of our soldiers must be provided for to the fullest extent, but that provision must follow the laws of system and the maximum of efficiency, if the work is to be done without waste and indirection.

Problems that arise from the assembling of great numbers of men in the service in any one locality must be dealt with without delay and with the foresight and directness that are possible only to cooperative intelligence as well as to cooperative love.

The tasks, therefore, which face the Church are countless and the complications without number. In the nature of the case, duplication, delay, oversight and waste are forbidden. Men and women who have insight, imagination and courage must undertake the course of complicated thinking in order to guide the workers into pathways that prevent confusion and obviate all neutralization.

The National Catholic War Council was created, therefore, because these needs were apparent and because they permitted no delay and threatened an indictment of the Catholic Church unless they were met swiftly and efficiently. Whatever the limitations under which these efforts have been made, no one can deny that a great purpose inspired them. Whatever limitations that still adhere to the plans proposed, these plans have resulted from an unselfish endeavor to do a great duty in a noble manner. Neither the inspiration that created the National Catholic War Council nor the plans which it proposes will be understood except from a national standpoint and in a national way. These plans follow closely the established ecclesiastical order and action in Catholic life. The National Catholic War Council, therefore, aims frankly towards the amalgamation of all these forces and towards the studying of those larger problems in the Church which will enable her now to meet her historic responsibilities.

The Church in the United States has need of accurate knowledge of the problems presented to her by war conditions. She has need of the knowledge of her own resources, which may be called upon to deal with these problems. On account of her vastness, the variety of her life, and the manifold character of the units of Catholic feeling and action, there is imperative need of system, of foresight and of direction. By the law of her life and the sanctions of her history, all such efforts must center around her normal authorities. We turn to pastors for guidance in parochial problems.

We turn to bishops for guidance in diocesan problems. We turn to the Hierarchy for guidance in national problems.

The National Catholic War Council is the Hierarchy, and the Committee on Special War Activities serves the Bishops in whatever way they may be disposed to ask. It keeps in touch with all diocesan war councils, and thus, indirectly, with all parochial units within the diocese.

Sharing as we do the inspiration of divine Faith; feeling as we do the impulse of a patriotism that is quickened by our belief in the supernatural, we are assured that the problem of placing the Church in a position of recognized power in dealing with war conditions is one of good will, not of resources; one of organization, not of choice; one of privilege gladly seized. Prompt surrender, therefore, of all local or sectional points of view, glad obedience to our national, spiritual and civic ideals, and hearty understanding of the elementary truth that system and forethought are the weapons by which we overcome confusion and wasted effort, stand today as the sole factors under the Providence of God, which condition our meeting the supreme challenge that has come to us, meeting it in a way that will make the country forever grateful, and the Church forever proud.

CHAPTER II

THE CATHOLIC ARMY AND NAVY CHAPLAIN BUREAU

CHAPTER II

THE CATHOLIC ARMY AND NAVY CHAPLAIN BUREAU

BISHOP ORDINARY

RT. REV. PATRICK J. HAYES, D. D., Auxiliary Bishop of New York. Address, 142 East 29th Street, New York City.

Secretary, Rev. Joseph P. Dineen, Major, Chaplain 69th Infantry, New York Guard. Address, 142 E. 29th Street, New York City.

Executive Secretary, Rev. Lewis J. O'Hern, C. S. P. Address, 932 14th Street, Washington, D. C.

Vicars General:

Overseas Vicariate, VERY REV. MSGR. JAMES N. CONNOLLY, Major, Chaplain 12th Infantry, New York Guard. Address, 1—3 Rue des Italiens, Paris, France.

Eastern Vicariate, VERY REV. GEORGE J. WARING, Captain, 11th Cavalry, U. S. A. Address, Governor's Island, New York.

Great Lakes Vicariate, VERY REV. WILLIAM M. FOLEY. Address, 1012 E. 47th Street, Chicago, Illinois.

Gulf Vicariate, VERY REV. LESLIE J. KAVANAUGH. Address, 2432 Napoleon Avenue, New Orleans.

Pacific Coast Vicariate, VERY REV. JOSEPH M. GLEASON, Palo Alto, Cal.

NATIONAL CATHOLIC WAR COUNCIL

In the years of national peace which for so long blessed our country the question of chaplains for our Army and Navy while an important one was not of wide range. In 1905 the Archbishops of the United States authorized the late Very Reverend Alexander P. Doyle, C. S. P. to act as their representative with the Government in the appointment of Catholic chaplains. In these days the chaplains were obliged to procure their faculties from the Bishop of the diocese in which they were stationed.

Father Doyle devoted himself heart and soul to this work until his untimely death in 1912. The Reverend Louis J. O'Hern, C. S. P., was appointed his successor and filled the post most meritoriously until the outbreak of the present war. The vast number of Catholic chaplains needed for war service, the government and administration of what may be called the "Army and Navy Service" which they form, demanded the appointment of a Bishop with full jurisdiction. The Holy Father in November, 1918, appointed the Right Reverend Patrick J. Hayes as Bishop Ordinary of all Catholic chaplains of the United States. The approval of candidates, the care and government of all Catholic chaplains both at home and abroad are now under the immediate jurisdiction of Bishop Hayes. Bishop Hayes within a very short period has shown not only his zeal but an unusual gift of organization. He has established an Overseas vicariate under the direction of Msgr. Connolly which shortly will be subdivided with vicar generals in France, England and Italy. He divided our country into four vicariates. In the East Chaplain Waring, U. S. A., Captain in the 11th Cavalry, and who as a Catholic Chaplain in the Regular Army before the war devoted years of time and effort toward better chaplain service in the Army, has over charge of the Eastern Vicariate. The Great Lake District or Central West is given in charge of Vicar General Foley. The South and the Gulf states are under the care of Vicar General Kavanaugh, and the Far West and Pacific Coast under Vicar General Gleason.

Bishop Hayes has just returned from a visitation to all the camps of this country; he is now about to start on a journey overseas where he will visit personally the entire Allied battle front.

CHAPTER III

FORMATION OF DIOCESAN WAR COUNCILS

CHAPTER III

FORMATION OF DIOCESAN WAR COUNCILS

Plan of Organization. War problems in the Diocese. Duties of the different Diocesan Standing Committees. Suggested methods of cooperation with the National Committees. Cooperative Work of the Parishes.

The National Catholic War Council touches every diocese and every national Catholic activity, and the hope is that through the Diocesan War Council every Catholic man and woman will be interested in, and informed about, the work of cooperation. It is the desire of the National Catholic War Council that not only in every Diocese, but also in every parish in the country, a Catholic War Council Committee be established.

1. SUGGESTED PLANS FOR ORGANIZATION

The following suggestions are offered as being in general among the most practical for securing effective work in the diocese and cooperation with the national body. It is impossible to give detailed directions that would fit the various diocesan conditions. The Bishops of each diocese will know what best answers the needs and the resources of his own diocese. Our suggestions therefore are as follows. The head of the Diocesan War Council is of course the Bishop of the Diocese. He may associate with himself as his Council, a Vice-President, a Secretary and a Treasurer. It is advisable to have the Diocesan Council operate through an Executive Committee of priests and laymen and women appointed by the Bishop. This Executive Committee will relieve the Bishops of the immediate problems of the war relief and will, under him, have supervision of all Standing Committees of the Diocesan War Council. To bring the whole diocese into active interest, a General Committee might be constituted of representative men and women appointed by each pastor, subject to the approval of the Bishop.

The immediate personal direction of the Bishop is the foundation on which the Diocesan War Council rests. In its proposed work of assembling and directing the resources of the diocese for war work, the War Council ought to have in mind two things: First, the realization of the demands for civic and Catholic war service; second, the adjustment of the work of the diocese with that of other sections of the Church in the United States in so far as the gigantic problems of war demand unity and coordination. The Diocesan War Council will be in intimate touch with all Diocesan life. It alone is in position to give satisfactory direction to these war activities. The Diocesan War Council can gain a national outlook by coordinating its activities to the National Catholic War Council.

There is not a Catholic parish in the United States from which young men have not gone to the service of the country, placing life itself in jeopardy for the defense of the flag. There is not a Catholic parish in the United States whose spirit has not been quickened and whose affections have not bravely followed the soldiers and sailors wherever duty has called them. There are no national and perhaps few, if any, local organizations that have not already undertaken many duties in war work in a spirit of self-forgetting patriotism. There is not a diocese from which material, spiritual and moral resources have not flowed in steady streams toward camp or battlefield or battleship where soldiers and sailors are prepared to fight in our defense. All of this is precious but perhaps incomplete. Questions have arisen from many sides as to the direction of the activity of our Catholic forces. Many have felt that what was done was good in itself and greatly to be admired, but that it seemed to lack the touch of a larger organization and a central purpose through which alone it might find its fullest voice. Organizations, leaders and localities have demanded some kind of uniformity of direction which would give us common terms by which to state our duties, to measure our activities and to meet our responsibilities with promptness and accurateness.

In some sections of the country, Catholic activity tends to merge itself into larger civic and social movements that have already been so rich in promise and so glorious in achievement. In other localities, endeavor has been made not only to give wholesome cooperation to approved civic and social movements but also to arouse Catholic instinct for distinctive Catholic effort in following the soul of the soldier as well as body, feeling and mind as he went to the front. In certain localities, a tendency has developed to confine war activities to the service of soldiers and sailors who have gone from city or diocese, without rising to the concept of our national problems as a whole. This development has not brought the full inspiration of national purpose and the unity of national ideal into play. National organizations can undertake tasks only in a national way, and anything else involves partial results, duplication of appeal, and failure to link resources into an effective system. Furthermore, cities near which camps are found may be overwhelmed by material, social, moral and civic problems. In those sections, Catholics may feel utterly at a loss to deal with those phases of camp life which the Government leaves free to voluntary effort. On the other hand, there are localities rich in resources but far removed from camp life and camp problems. Something is needed to coordinate all these resources in a definite and complete way, in order that help toward the complete adjustment of national Catholic life to national civic problems may be given.

At the outset of the war, noble expressions of a unified concept of the nation's problems and of the Church's impulse to do her part came from the Hierarchy. Equally admirable expressions of these same points of view came from scholars and from lay and clerical leaders; but the action of the Church as one great factor in the nation's life and the coordination of its efforts and the direction of its resources lack that unity which is the symbol of power.

The plan of organization presented in this Handbook for Diocesan War Council work is based upon the organization of the Church of the United States. It embraces all the lines of activities that may be taken up in any given locality. It is true that the dioceses where there are no camps or cantonments have not the same immediate problems as the others. Naturally, the presence of a camp or cantonment in a diocese creates problems that are local only geographically, but in a moral, spiritual and civic sense, national problems must be dealt with by every diocese from a national outlook. If soldiers from five States of fifteen dioceses are found in a single cantonment, the problems created concern the entire Church of the country and not simply the dioceses in question. There are many dioceses in which no problems present themselves directly, but there is no diocese exempt from this supreme appeal to the Church to meet every responsibility that confronts her with uncalculating enthusiasm.

The majority of soldiers are in Southern camps. Here problems are at a maximum and Catholic resources are at a minimum. Only a national outlook on the situation can marshall our resources in an orderly way and secure the full expression of Catholic devotion with far-reaching results.

It would be impossible for a hundred or more dioceses, for as many bishops and many million Catholics to coordinate resources and action with adequate effect unless an agency were created to unify effort and to suggest the essentials of satisfactory cooperation.

That agency is the National Catholic War Council and its representative in every diocese is the Diocesan War Council. The Standing Committees, therefore, of all diocesan war activities may be patterned after those of the national body. To illustrate the work of cooperation between the dioceses and the national organization the following paragraphs are given as suggested outlines for diocesan war work.

2. COOPERATIVE COMMITTEES OF THE DIOCESAN WAR COUNCIL

A. THE DIOCESAN FINANCE COMMITTEE

The duty of this Committee is to perfect a financial organization of the diocese in such a way that when a drive for funds, either diocesan or national, is to be made, the Ordinary will have at his command a Committee ready to carry out the work. Much of the care to be given Catholic soldiers from populous dioceses will devolve upon localities where the Catholics are few in number, and the good work of these sparsely-settled communities must be sustained by the generosity of the Catholic people from all parts of the nation. The Diocesan Finance Committee should consist of a group of men and women having a complete and intimate knowledge of the parishes of the diocese and thoroughly acquainted with methods of making collections for drives. All local teams to be organized for such purpose should be under the direction of this Committee. Heads of societies in each diocese should be brought together and made acquainted with the plans of the Finance Committee, and their hearty cooperation should be enlisted from the beginning.

B. THE WOMEN'S ACTIVITIES COMMITTEE OF THE DIOCESE

The program of activities for the Diocesan Women's Committee embraces a thorough examination of present conditions of Catholic Women's organizations in the Diocese, their purpose, their numerical strength, their normal activities, and their value with regard to war work. Efforts should be made to combine these local societies into a Diocesan Committee of Women's Activities. This would coordinate the work and prevent a duplication of effort and give greater facility in meeting the diocesan needs. It is hardly necessary to add that as a result of this the distinctive work of each society will be strengthened through this cooperation.

The following methods of war relief for Catholic Women's Societies are suggested:

I. Affiliation with

a. American Red Cross.

b. Women's Committee, Council of National Defense.

c. Food Administration.

d. Local civic war agencies

In every instance Catholic interests can be better served and Catholic women's war service more widely directed and effectively administered through cordial cooperation with government and non-religious agencies. Catholic units do not thereby lose their identity but are accorded full credit for all work done, and Catholic cooperation is eagerly welcomed by these organizations.

II. Cooperation in all civic movements for the stimulation of war interests—example:

a. Increase Red Cross membership.

b. Patriotic food exhibits.

c. Advancement of food conservation program.

d. Liberty Loan parades.

An adequate appreciation of what Catholics are doing can be obtained by a willing interest in all such ventures as indicated above. It is an effective way to dissipate criticism and to break down prejudice and suspicion.

III. Secure representation on every war activity or committee in the city.

Such representation will be cheerfully afforded when the request has been advanced with proper authority. This affords opportunity for a wider application of Catholic principles to the problems arising out of war relief.

IV. Cooperation with Travelers' Aid Society or the establishment of an equivalent relief where none exists.

The large increase in traveling on the part of soldiers' wives, sisters and mothers and the general movement on the part of women war workers has emphasized the need of Travelers' Aid, and Catholic participation in such work will mean the protection and relief of many Catholic girls.

V. Cooperation in the Big Sister movement or the encouragement of such activity where it does not exist.

The natural sympathy of the young girl for the man in uniform and the wider opportunity for amusement makes it imperative that detailed supervision of young girls should be undertaken.

VI. The establishment of committees to keep informed of government needs for women employees and the spread of this information.

Women workers are in great demand by the Government at present and with the drafting of so many young men from civil employment into the Army, a wider and wider field of labor is opened up for women. A real service can be done the Government and the individual by keeping informed of the needs of employer and employee.

VII. Proper housing of girl war workers.

In most centers throughout the country, the demand for the woman laborer has created a serious problem by throwing into unprepared communities a large number of young women. The problem of securing proper housing and proper amusement for these workers is most serious and pressing. Where at all possible, individual service in this regard should be afforded.

VIII. To exercise interest and direction in the formation and development of girls' clubs.

The general movement toward such organizations outside the Church makes it necessary that some such provision be afforded Catholics if we are to fulfill our duties as Catholics to the Government.

IX. Visiting military hospitals at regular intervals, providing fruit and delicacies, reading matter, cheerful conversation.

The large number of sick and wounded who are away from home associates find homesickness and loneliness real hindrances to their recovery. The cheerful kindly visitor can do much to lighten the weariness of these men and be most helpful toward war service.

X. To seek service as canteen workers where such agencies are established by non-religious organizations.

As this form of service has been carried out in many places, Dallas, St. Louis, Pittsburgh, it is another opportunity for manifesting a spirit of cooperation and of bringing Catholic influence into non-Catholic grounds.

XI. To provide a light breakfast for soldiers receiving Holy Communion and who would, otherwise, be deprived of this meal.

In many camps and cantonments, this has proved a very needed and interesting service and many chaplains have urged it as the most practical form of serving relief to Catholic men. Where adequate arrangements can be made with the Government to supply breakfast outside of regular hours this, of course, should be done.

C. THE MEN'S ACTIVITIES COMMITTEE OF THE DIOCESE

The duty of the Men's Activities Diocesan Committee is a varied one. It has the responsibility of harnessing every activity that will tend to improve the moral and spiritual welfare of the enlisted man, and at the same time provide for him wholesome and innocent recreation. Among these activities, the following may be mentioned:

I. *Religious Work.*

a. To see that a sufficient number of Masses is provided for all Catholic soldiers and sailors within the training camps. To see that notices are posted at camps and railroad stations regarding the nearest Catholic Churches in the cities adjoining the camps, together with the hours of Masses. In communities where pamphlets are issued, giving information to enlisted men, the committee should see that Catholic Churches are mentioned therein, their location, and the hours of Masses.

b. If no branch of the Catholic Big Brother Movement is established in the locality a sub-committee should be appointed, charged with looking after the boys whose fathers are in the service.

c. To assist the St. Vincent de Paul Society in its work among the poor. It can be reasonably expected that war conditions will impose greater responsibility on this organization.

d. To assist the local authorities in suppressing places that are dangerous to the morals of the soldiers. All Catholic agencies should be actively employed in cooperating with the civic authorities in this matter. This ought not to be left to chance, but should constitute a definite part of the activities of the Men's Committee.

II. *Recreation Work.*

a. The Committee on Men's Activities should provide wholesome and innocent recreation for the soldiers, by encouraging all Catholic organizations to throw open their doors to enlisted men and also to provide special entertainment for them. The parish halls should be utilized for these special entertainments.

b. The list of automobile owners should be made with a view of holding sight-seeing trips for enlisted men. A list of entertainers should be compiled with a view of furnishing special entertainments in the camps.

c. Contests of an athletic nature between teams representing the camps and parish organizations might be arranged.

d. Magazines and periodicals should be collected to be forwarded to the training camps, also sheet music, music rolls, and phonograph records.

e. The Knights of Columbus should be assisted in securing capable secretaries for the work at home, in the camps, and abroad.

f. A Speakers' Bureau made up of the best Catholic men to go from parish to parish and arouse an interest and enthusiasm in the work of the Council.

g. A Central Bureau of Information should be established for enlisted men to obtain advice and direction. This Bureau should be advertised in the camps and in railroad stations.

h. Sleeping quarters for enlisted men who are on a visit to the city should be provided wherever possible.

i. A list of boarding houses where Catholic men can obtain accommodations in Catholic surroundings should be advertised.

The problems created by the presence of so many soldiers in cities near camps and cantonments is as serious, in its way, as that of the care of men who are fighting at the front. Catholic men of patriotic zeal have many avenues of activity opened up to them by this problem, whether they are residents of such cities or far away from the same. Today the soldier is everywhere. His wants touch every citizen. The Diocesan Committee on Men's Activities is a centralizing and directing agency for all the Catholics and for the Catholic organizations of the diocese. Upon it depends to a large extent whether or not the Catholic Church receives her due share of praise for the work the faithful are doing in furthering the great ends of the war.

D. DIOCESAN COMMITTEE ON HISTORICAL RECORDS

The purpose of the Diocesan Committee on Historical Records shall be to act as a central board in directing the work of collecting war history material throughout the diocese. It should prepare programs of activity for the use of parochial committee on historical records. It should direct by correspondence and by personal visit the kind of material to be collected and suggest plans for its being sent to the National Catholic Archives at Washington. All historical material concerning Catholic activity in the diocese should be collected, preserved, filed and properly indexed; one copy should be placed in the Diocesan Archives, and another copy sent to the National Committee on Historical Records, at 932 14th street, N. W., Washington, D. C.

It would be well to have appointed in each ecclesiastical center someone to take charge of the local Catholic papers, and Catholic press clippings should be made of every item in any way pertaining to the history of Catholic war activity in the diocese. Prizes should be offered on such subjects as the diocesan records in the war, and a grand prize should be offered for the best written history of diocesan activity, to be given at the close of the war so as to stimulate the pupils of the parochial schools and the colleges to be on the lookout for all historical material.

The one main duty, however, of the Diocesan Committee on Historical Records is to complete a census of the men who have entered the service. Cards or blanks should be sent broadcast to the families in the diocese, asking for the name and home address of each soldier, his branch of service, and the name of his nearest relative. A file should be kept of all promotions, honors, decorations, etc., given to the men in the service from the diocese. A Casualty List of the diocese should also be kept. Copies of all these lists should be filed with the Chancellor of the diocese and with the National Committee at Washington.

E. DIOCESAN COMMITTEE ON CHAPLAINS' AID

Every diocese should constitute itself a Chapter of the Chaplains' Aid Association. Chaplains' outfits, New Testaments, Prayer Books, Rosaries, Scapulars, Medals, Catechisms, Religious Pamphlets, Tracts on Social Hygiene and on General Health, Religious Books, Magazines, Periodicals, Crucifixes, etc., etc., are some of the things needed in every Regiment, and on every warship of our Forces. The entire Church in the United States must meet these demands, and every parish in the country should be united into the Diocesan Chapter for the work to be successful. It will be to the everlasting credit of the diocese if, after the war, its part in this laudable portion of war service has been in proportion to its numbers and to its wealth.

3. NATIONAL AND DIOCESAN COOPERATION

The National Catholic War Council does not interfere in any way in Diocesan Local war activities, but leaves to them a full scope. It offers its service to these diocesan war councils and is most willing to render any assistance in its power to supply local needs or to remedy defects. This cooperation can only be accomplished through the Ordinary of the Diocese. From him all activities find their normal origin. Through his zeal and cooperation alone can success come to organized effort.

4. COOPERATIVE WORK OF THE PARISHES

It will be seen that this work of the national organization seeks to bring into coordinated service all the resources of the Church in the United States. For its full completion we must reach every individual Catholic. To achieve that it is not sufficient to have a National Catholic War Council and a Diocesan War Council in every diocese. The entire flock must actually support their shepherd, the parishes must zealously cooperate under the leadership of their Bishop.

The parish is the supreme testing place for the length and breadth and depth of Catholic patriotism. It is from the parish that the Diocesan War Council must expect its most thorough cooperation. Apart from the patriotic motive which must inspire these parochial units, there is another reason that should appeal very strongly to the pastor and people: The world will never be the same after this great war, for there is something more than political ideas at stake. This war is a war of Christian morality against pagan materialism, and there is a greater crisis to come in the moral world after the war is over than in the political or economic world. The world is fighting its way back to Christianity and to Christian moral principles and unless a strong public opinion in recognition of the sacrifices of the Catholic Church of the United States has been created, discrimination, lack of confidence and probably open opposition will later result. It is needless to emphasize that in the perfection of Catholic organization the parochial unit is the heart of all Catholic endeavor. To an already over-burdened clergy, the National Catholic War Council must look for inspiration, for response, and for patriotic self-sacrifice.

Governmental agencies are making a distinction between strictly denominational work and cooperative work. The strictly denominational work of the Catholic Church during the present war is hardly more than a strengthening and vitalizing of the agencies already in existence. Among these, may be mentioned the St. Vincent de Paul's Society, the Holy Name Society and the Sodalities of the Blessed Virgin. These three bodies will be kindled with new zeal in their religious life, since it is taking on a new aspect through the inspiration of patriotic effort. These societies will become stronger; their membership will become greater; their individual and cooperative work more intense and more constant. In this strictly Catholic work, the activities of these different societies have the inherent capacity for growth, and they can do very much without in any way infringing upon the work of the Committee for Men's Activities. In this strictly Catholic parochial war work, the pastor is not only the leader and guide, but it is from him that the inspiration for all such activity must come. The spiritual side of the war, that side which has been so eloquently represented in the letters of our Holy Father Benedict XV, and in his prayers for peace, can here find a proper field. The religious side of the war should be brought home constantly to the men who are members of the Holy Name Society, and their meetings should be made, as far as possible, to center around the great ideal of prayer for the boys who are at the front, and especially for peace. The sodalities should be made to understand the preeminent place the devotion of the Mother of God has had in the great crises of the past. They need only be told of that crisis which came in the third quarter of the sixteenth century, when civilization met a great enemy in the Turk, and how at the battle of Lepanto it was the prayers of Catholic Europe to the Blessed Mother which brought the world victory from its foes. They need only be told of the place the Rosary has held all through the centuries in winning victory after victory for the Catholic nations of the past. The members of the St. Vincent de Paul Society need only to open those pages of the history of France which tell of the awful chaos of the French Revolution to find inspiration and stimulus for the new activities that can justly be attempted by them. The parish itself as a body can be made into a community of prayer for guidance for the President and the members of his cabinet, for the members of Congress, for the leaders of the Army and Navy, and for all those who are guiding the United States on to victory.

To suggest methods of war activities for all parishes of the United States would be to go into a too lengthy detailed statement of what the country is asking of its citizens at the present time. The main, important thing to be said in this respect is that every parish must realize that the work they must do in the present war will, undoubtedly, be continued for many years. The parish must awake to the fact that it has a responsibility not only within its own boundary lines, but to the nation at large and to the Church at large. The formation of a national body such as the National Catholic War Council does not relieve the parish of its responsibilities, nor does it lessen its program of intelligent cooperation with the governmental agencies of war service.

In each parish of the diocese wherever practical, and the Bishop so directs, a Parochial War Council should be established with the Pastor as the head. In forming it he may with advantage follow as far as possible the outline with regard to the Parochial Executive Committee and the Parochial Standing Committees which has been suggested above for Diocesan War Councils. Every Parochial War Council when formed is of course under the supervision of its Diocesan War Council.

When thus organized, the parochial war units of the diocese have it in their power, therefore, to form a strong central organization in which no single aspect of war service will be denied its legitimate place. These units should endeavor to seek out all existing forces in the parish and to bring them into intelligent and sympathetic relationship, so that all waste and friction and inefficiency may be avoided. These units should be so thoroughly one in spirit and in method that the Diocesan War Council may be prepared to give adequate cooperation in the new problems of war service and reconstruction which may have to be faced when the war is over.

CHAPTER IV

GOVERNMENTAL AND SUPPLEMENTAL AGENCIES IN WAR WOR

CHAPTER IV

GOVERNMENTAL AND SUPPLEMENTAL AGENCIES IN WAR WORK

1. NECESSITY OF COOPERATION

The war has mobilized every resource of the American nation for the one purpose of bringing victory to the ideals of the allied world. No individual in this great land of ours can stand without the circle of war-workers. From the moment that a state of war was declared between this country and Germany, the watch-word turned from preparedness to cooperation. Individual cooperation has been accepted by the Government whenever it has been found valuable. But it is the cooperation of organized bodies in the land which is best suited for the work the Government has outlined as its support. The Government has called first for cooperation with regard to the national needs of the different churches of the land. The situation in camp, in city, and in the army which has presented so many problems requiring good will and amicable consultation by representatives of the different churches, makes such cooperation imperative. Standing fully erect on the God-given platform of his divine faith, the Catholic not only may, but should cooperate in these great civic and patriotic measures which are common to us all as citizens. No one will deny that the most highly centralized religious body in the world as well as in every nation is the Catholic Church. With its perfect system of jurisdiction it is one of the most vital factors in the nation's life whether in time of war or in time of peace. The Catholic Church stands as the most stable moral force within the nation. Its moral principles are fundamental to every Christian problem which arises, and its federated responsibility renders it one of the efficacious means of cooperation with the definite program of war work which the Government has outlined.

The different Protestant denominations have organized for war purposes under the title "The General War-Time Commission of the Federal Churches of Christ in America:" the Jews, orthodox and reformed, under "The Jewish Welfare Board of the United States Army and Navy." The national organization for the war work of the Catholic Church is the "National Catholic War Council." All of these are asked to cooperate with governmental agencies on war work. The problems of the Government are in many cases common to all and only a common understanding can contribute to national well-being. It is our duty to manifest a spirit of cooperation in national and in local problems. And it is our duty also to cooperate with all the agencies of national war work that the Government has established.

It would be impossible to give a complete description of the governmental agencies; but a description of the principal ones will be sufficient to enable each distinct unit of the National Catholic War Council to find the best scope for its activities. In the following pages the chief governmental and social agencies are outlined, and the Chairmen of the different Committees of the Diocesan War Councils and of the parochial units will find these agencies at all times most willing to give direction and to assist in the work of speedy and accurate cooperation with their plans. The following statements have been in each case prepared by the officials of the agencies in question, and the National Catholic War Council desires to place here on historical record its appreciation of the courtesy with which their requests for these statements have been met.

2. THE PRINCIPAL AGENCIES OF COOPERATION
A. GOVERNMENTAL AGENCIES
I. DEPARTMENT OF THE TREASURY
Secretary of Treasury, HON. WILLIAM G. MCADOO
Bureau of War-Risk Insurance
Assistant Secretary, MR. THOMAS B. LOVE
(Address, Treasury Dept., Wash., D. C.)

What the United States Government does for its fighting men and their families.

The United States Government provides three forms of financial protection for its fighting forces and their families:

a. Allotments and Allowances.

Every *enlisted man* in the active military or naval service is under a duty to allot $15 a month from his pay to his wife and children. To these *compulsory allotments* the Government adds *family allowances*, ranging from $5 a month for a motherless child, and $15 for a wife without children, up to a maximum of $50. The compulsory allotments are the same for all enlisted men, regardless of rank or pay. Provision is also made covering instances of a divorced wife to whom alimony has been decreed and who has not remarried.

In addition to the compulsory allotments, the enlisted man may also make *voluntary allotments* to his parents, grandparents, brothers, sisters, or grandchildren, and, *if they are dependent upon him* for *support*, the Government may add certain monthly family allowances. Not more than $50 in family allowances will be paid on account of any one enlisted man.

If the enlisted man is already making a compulsory allotment to his wife and children, he need allot only $5 additional to his brothers, sisters, parents, grandparents, and grandchildren, if he desires a family allowance for them. But if he is not making a compulsory allotment, he must allot $15 to such other relatives to obtain a government allowance for them.

By this system of allotments and allowances the enlisted man and the Government together make provision for the loved ones left behind.

b. Compensation for Death or Disability.

This compensation is the modern American substitute for the pension. It applies to *officers and enlisted men alike* when employed in active service, regardless of rank or pay, and is payable for death or disability *incurred in the line of duty* and not caused by their own willful misconduct.

In case of *death*, compensation, which ranges from $20 to $75 a month, is paid to the soldier's or sailor's *widow, children, and dependent father or mother*. No other relatives are entitled to compensation. The compensation may be paid to a widow until remarriage, and to a child until the age of eighteen, or until marriage.

In case of *disability* compensation is payable to the disabled person himself. If the disability is *total*, the amount of compensation varies from $30 to $95 per month, according to the size of the disabled man's family. In exceptional cases a sum not exceeding $20 per month additional may be paid for services of a nurse.

If the disability is *partial*, the compensation is a percentage of the compensation that would be payable for total disability and the amount varies according to the size of the disabled person's family and the reduction in his earning capacity. In certain specific cases of total disability, such as the loss of both feet or both hands or both eyes, or for becoming helpless and permanently bedridden, compensation is payable at the rate of $100 per month.

Compensation for death and disability should be clearly distinguished from the *Government insurance protection*, which is entirely separate.

c. *Government Insurance.*

In addition to the compensation for death or disability, the United States offers its fighting forces the further protection of *Government insurance*. This insurance is protection against death or total permanent disability. It is granted on written application and the payment of premium to all persons in the active military or naval service, enlisted, enrolled, drafted, or commissioned. No medical examination is necessary other than a favorable report by the Army or Navy surgeon or medical examining board before acceptance by the military or naval forces. Because the Government bears all overhead expenses and the extra war hazard, the cost is extremely low. The terms are so favorable and the protection so broad that virtually all men joining the colors, both married and unmarried, with and without dependents, are eagerly taking the full amount—namely, $10,000. The premium rate depends on the man's age, and for the full $10,000 averages between $6 and $7 a month.

To obtain this Government insurance, the man must apply *within 120 days after he enters the active military or naval service.*

In case of death of a person having so applied for $10,000 insurance, the Government will pay, so long as there are persons living who are entitled to receive the same, monthly instalments of $57.50 each for twenty years, which, taking interest in account, aggregate $13,800. The insurance cannot be made payable to anyone except those included in the "permitted class," namely, spouse, child, grandchild, parent, brother, or sister, as defined in the War-Risk Insurance Act.

In case of *total permanent disability* these monthly installments of $57.50 each will be paid to the disabled person throughout his life even though he lives for more than twenty years.

Provision is made for the continuation of this *Government insurance* after leaving the service, and for its conversion under the provisions of the Act, *without medical examination*, not later than five years after the close of the war. In addition to its other advantages, therefore, this insurance, backed by all the resources of the United States Government, enables the fighting man to *insure his insurability*, regardless of his physical condition after the war.

These three forms of Government aid—allotments and allowances, compensation for death or disability, and United States Government insurance—are grouped together under the War-Risk Insurance Act, approved by the President on October 6, 1917, and administered, under the direction of the Secretary of the Treasury, by the Bureau of War-Risk Insurance.

This is the greatest measure of protection ever offered to its fighting forces by any nation in the history of the world. It is not charity; it is in the essence of justice to the gallant men who have gone to the colors, and to their loved ones at home. It strengthens America's fighting forces as they go forth to battle; it safeguards the families left behind; and by its broad and generous provisions it takes from war its chief terror—fear for the future.

In addition to administering the War-Risk Insurance Act, the Bureau of War-Risk Insurance is authorized to act for men in the active military service, under the provision of the Soldiers' and Sailors' Civil Relief Act, approved March 8, 1918, in the matter of the lapsing or forfeiture of certain specified life insurance contracts, either in life insurance companies or fraternal orders or organizations.

If the Government guarantees to the insurance company or organization the payment of premiums, the policy will remain in force, and the man in service will have one year after the end of military service in which to pay any defaulted premiums, before the policy or membership lapses.

The benefits of the Soldiers' and Sailors' Civil Relief Act are available only upon application. The act applies only to persons in the service from March 8, 1918 (the date of the approval of the act), and to persons entering active service after that date, from such date of entry.

The insurance under the Soldiers' and Sailors' Civil Relief Act does not apply to Government insurance issued by the Bureau of War Risk Insurance.

Persons having business with the Bureau of War-Risk Insurance can help themselves and increase the efficiency of the Bureau very materially in the following ways:

1. By giving all the necessary information in their letters, including their own full names and post-office addresses, and the name, rank, and organization of the soldier or sailor concerning whom they are writing.

2. By using a clear, legible hand-writing—if necessary, print hand-writing. Give full names always; initials are not enough.

3. By addressing all claims for compensation, allowances, or insurance, directly to the Bureau of War-Risk Insurance. *It is unnecessary to employ claim agents.*

4. By promptly notifying the Bureau of all changes in family status.

5. By giving the allotment number in all correspondence concerning allotments and allowances.

6. By remembering that allotments and allowances are not payable the same month in which they are made. Allotments from July pay, for example, are not

due until August. Persons remembering this will save themselves unnecessary worry, and the Bureau unnecessary correspondence.

7. By urging their relatives and friends who are in the military and naval service of the Nation to avail themselves promptly of the full $10,000 Government Insurance protection. The time within which application can be made is strictly limited by law to within 120 days after the man joins the service.

8. By remembering that allotments are compulsory only for the wife and children of an enlisted man, including a former wife divorced, who has not remarried, and to whom alimony has been decreed. Allotments for parents, grandparents, grandchildren, brothers and sisters, are voluntary, and Government allowances will be granted to these relative only in cases of dependency, provided the necessary allotments are made by the enlisted man.

Additional literature, detailed information, and the necessary application blanks concerning any or all features of the War-Risk Insurance Act may be had by writing to the Bureau of War-Risk Insurance, Treasury Department, Washington, D. C.

II. DEPARTMENT OF WAR AND NAVY
Secretary of War, HON. NEWTON D. BAKER
Secretary of Navy, HON. JOSEPHUS M. DANIELS

Commissions on Training Camp Activities

Chairman, MR. RAYMOND B. FOSDICK
Secretary, MR. W. PRENTICE SANGER
(Address: 19th and G streets, N. W., Washington, D. C.)

President Wilson has stated that he does not believe it an exaggeration to say that no army and navy ever before assembled have had more conscientious and painstaking thought given to the protection and stimulation of their mental, moral and physical manhood than the American armies at the present time, and that in this work The Commissions on Training Camp Activities are to be given the credit for the wonderful success attained so far.

The Commissions on Training Camp Activities have their offices at 19th and G Streets, N. W., Washington, D. C. Mr. Raymond B. Fosdick is Chairman of these Committees.

The twin Commissions on Training Camp Activities—one for the War Department and one for the Navy Department—which were appointed by Secretary Baker and Secretary Daniels early in the war, are charged with the responsibility of cultivating and conserving the manhood and manpower of America's fighting forces. By a comprehensive recreational and educational program, and by strict enforcement of vice and liquor laws, the Commissions aim to surround the men in service with an environment which is not only clean and wholesome but positively inspiring—the kind of environment which a democracy owes to those who fight in its behalf.

When one considers that the hundreds of thousands of men who are pouring into army and navy camps have left behind them their families, friends, clubs, church and college gatherings, their dances, their athletic fields, their theatres and town libraries—in fact all the normal social relationships to which they have been accustomed—and have entered the bewildering environment of a war camp, the absolute need of some sort of substitute becomes apparent. Contentment for the average man cannot be maintained without the normal relationships of life, and it is only a contented army and navy which is in real fighting trim.

That is why the Government has supplied, through the Commissions and through the organizations which they coordinate, abundant recreation in the form of theatrical entertainment, athletics, mass singing, club life, educational opportunities within camps, and organized hospitality in war camp communities. The Commissions' athletic directors, boxing instructors, song leaders, theatre managers and dramatic entertainment coaches, who are on the payroll of the Government, together with the thousands of representatives of the Y. M. C. A., Knights of Columbus, Jewish Welfare Board, American Library Association, Y. W. C. A. and War Camp Community Service, are busy today ministering to the social needs of the million and a half men training in our camps. And behind it all is one big purpose—*to win the war.*

Such are the diversions which the Commissions set up to compete with those harmful attractions traditionally associated with training camps. The other side of the Commissions' activities is found in their work of law enforcement and social hygiene education which is aimed directly to prevent spread of venereal disease—a factor which, as is well known, is most destructive of military efficiency. The War and Navy Departments at the very outbreak of war took the position that alcohol and the prostitute must be kept absolutely away from the soldier and sailor. The Law Enforcement and Social Hygiene Divisions of the Commissions' work act in cooperation with various agencies to suppress these evils.

The Twin Commissions on Training Camp Activities have divided their work into two sections: Leisure Time Activities inside the Camps and Leisure Time Activities outside the Camp. The Leisure Time Activities inside the Camps are being directed by the Y. M. C. A., by the K. of C. and by other organizations, such as the Jewish Welfare Board and the American Library Association. These activities include athletics, singing, general entertainment, theatricals, moving pictures and educational work. The Leisure Time Activities outside the Camps are being directed by the War Camp Community Service Commission. The Catholic clergy and in particular the Diocesan Committee on Men's Activities are urged to contribute as much of their time as possible to the work of the War Camp Community Service. This work is being directed by the Playground and Recreation Association of America. Its aim is to stimulate a wholesome friendliness between civilians in community near camps and the fighting men. The definite accomplishments of the War Camp Community Service fall naturally into five divisions:

1. Community Service.

Information bureaus, hotels, lodgings and restaurants have been opened for the men in service.

2. Community Hospitality.

Hundreds of clubs are maintained where a man's uniform is the only pass necessary. Community houses and social centers are operated. Dances, suppers and banquets, excursions and sight-seeing trips are planned. The

"Take a Soldier or Sailor Home to Dinner" movement, under the supervision of the trained workers of the War Camp Community Service, has become an enthusiasm throughout the country. The Commissions on Training Camp Activities endorse home hospitality under these circumstances.

3. *Community Amusement.*

Town pageants, festivals and parades are arranged for the men. Commercial amusements are supervised to see that the men get only the best and most wholesome for their money.

4. *Community Organization.*

To provide the men in training with the right kind of leisure-time recreation, the resources of clubs, fraternal bodies, chambers of commerce, boards of trade, churches and similar organizations are mobilized by the War Camp Community Service.

5. *Community Betterment.*

In many towns petty profiteering has been eliminated by the War Camp Community Service. "Square Deal" associations and "Better Business" bureaus have been formed. In general, the slogan of the camp city is not "What can we get out of the man in service?" but "What can we do for him?"

The work of the War Camp Community Service is vital. *Preservation of normal social relationship between the people and the men in training is an essential part of our military program.* The War Camp Community Service accomplishes this preservation. The Commissions discourage sentimentality toward the soldier and sailor, but they encourage attractive and healthful diversions. These are the things which American municipalities owe to the Nation's fighting men.

III. DEPARTMENT OF AGRICULTURE
Secretary of Agriculture, HON. DAVID R. HOUSTON
States Relations Service
Director, MR. A. C TRUE

(Address: Dept. of Agriculture, The Mall, Washington, D. C.)

Food production and food conservation are immediately and increasingly necessary for the prosecution of the war. Through the annihilation of nations and the employment of all able-bodied men to fight the common enemy, production has decreased, while the submarines have put vast continents out of consideration as a source of food. At present the United States and Canada stand alone as defenders against the world's food shortage. Hungry people lose courage. A serious food shortage in England, France or Italy increases the danger that their people may demand a premature peace and the consequent disaster to the ideals for which our armies fight.

With the boys of your own church in France, laying down their lives for our liberty, and the liberty of all peoples, we look to you as the leader of your people to assist those agencies working in your community to increase the world's food supply. May we suggest as the best means whereby you may effectively cooperate in this cause, that, if you are not already in touch with them, you get acquainted with your county agricultural agent, county (woman) home demonstration agent, and county boys' and girls' club leader. If you do not have their names they can be secured by addressing the Director of Agricultural Extension at your State Agricultural College. If you will express your interest in their work and your willingness to be of assistance these local leaders in food production and conservation will be only too glad to avail themselves of your aid and to consult with you.

The present situation gives a peculiar religious significance to the production and conservation of food. Good agriculture is basically religious. The farmer is a co-worker with God in answering the peoples' prayer for daily bread. In this common cause of religion and patriotism we are looking to the clergy of the United States not only for spiritual leadership, but for their influence and activity in the Various movements and measures being promoted by the cooperating national, state and county organizations. Your vision may focus and your leadership may radiate and inspire those ideals and attitudes in your people which will result in the consecration of their whole lives to the cause of freedom for which we fight.

We are asking the clergy of the United States to inform themselves thoroughly with regard to what is being done and what may be done in their own communities towards food production and conservation, and to assist by giving their powerful support to the agencies promoting the agricultural production program of their local communities.

The war may be won or lost by our ability to furnish food. Our duty is absolute. We count upon your help.

The Office of Home Economics is a part of the States Relations Service and is engaged in the study of problems relating to food, clothing, household equipment, and household labor, and the dissemination of information on these subjects by printed documents and in other ways. As a result of the war situation attention has been centered very largely upon food and its economical use, in conformity with the general food situation. In this work we have endeavored to interest housekeepers in food problems and to help them in meeting them. In connection with our work we have also carried on an extensive food survey in homes and public institutions, in which we have asked housekeepers to collect statistical data regarding food consumed in their families. This a considerable number have been willing to do and among the public institutions helping have been a number of Roman Catholic schools. Our mailing lists include many of your convent schools and the letters we have received regarding the material sent leads us to believe that our bulletins and charts have been found useful.

In carrying on the work of the Office of Home Economics we have endeavored to keep in touch with teachers and other leaders in home economics work by means of publications, correspondence, etc.

The Office of Extension Work in the North and West and the Office of Extension Work in the South are also parts of the States Relations Service and the Office of Home Economics endeavors so to shape its work that it can provide information which can be used by these offices, which are engaged in extension teaching in agriculture and home economics and come more directly in contact with the people in country and town than does the Office of Home Economics. Individuals and organizations can help on food conservation work by working with the extension people and can be helped in the work by using such bulletins and other printed documents as are issued by this office.

IV. DEPARTMENT OF LABOR
Secretary of Labor, HON. WILLIAM B. WILSON

A. United States Housing Corporation

Director, MR. OTTO M. EIDLITZ
Manager, MR. JAMES FORD
(Address: 1712 G Street, N. W., Washington, D. C.)

Catholic organizations can cooperate with this bureau by calling to its attention housing or other social needs of any community engaged on war contracts. Local cases of rent profiteering should be reported to the Homes Registration and Information Division of this bureau.

The Bureau of Industrial Housing and Transportation of the Department of Labor (613 G Street, N. W., Washington, D. C.) was established in February, 1918, to provide for the housing of labor in war industries.

The United States Housing Corporation was incorporated on July 11, to carry on all the new construction of the Bureau.

Adequate labor supply cannot be secured and held at centers of ordnance manufacture unless the workmen and their families can have reasonable dwellings. The function of the Bureau of Industrial Housing and Transportation is therefore, to arrange for housing labor employed on Army and Navy contracts; by

I. Discovering and listing all vacant dwellings and rooms, and organizing local Homes Registration Service.

II. Opening up the suburbs through improved transportation facilities.

III. Construction of new temporary or permanent dwellings, and by building communities of houses where large operations are needed.

The chief officials of the Bureau are the following:
Director and President of the Corporation.—OTTO M. EIDLITZ.
Assistant Director and Vice-President of the Corporation.—J. D. LELAND, 3rd.
General Manager and Secretary of the Corporation.—B. L. FENNER.

All new construction is handled by the five divisions, having complete charge of the preparation of plans and specifications and layouts, establishing standards of design and construction and supervising all the plans and the construction by the local architects, engineers, town planners and contractors for each project:

B. Working Boys' Reserve.
Director, MR. WILLIAM E. HALL
(Address: 1712 G Street, N. W., Wash., D. C.)

The United States Boys' Working Reserve is a registered army of patriotic young men of the ages of 16 to 20 years, both inclusive, organized under the Employment Service of the United States Department of Labor, to help the nation win the war in field and in factory. Its history begins May 1917. In twelve months it has effected its organization in every State of the Union, including the District of Columbia, and in the Territory of Hawaii. Thousands of boys have enrolled into its membership.

The organization of the Reserve is by States, with a Federal State Director in charge of every State Division; the States are, usually, organized into County Units, with a County Director in charge of the Reserve work of the county. The County Director is responsible to the Federal State Director. The Federal State Director is responsible to the National Director in Washington. Enrollment is made through schools, libraries, and other organizations. Enrolling Officers, one or more, are appointed by the County Director for every high school in the county and are commissioned to their office by a national commission emanating from Washington and countersigned by the Federal State Director.

To enroll in the Reserve the young man applies to the Enrolling Officer of his school, or to his Reserve County Director, or to the Librarian of the

Public Library, or to his Association or finally to his Federal State Director. He fills out an enrollment card; obtains the consent of his parent or guardian; takes the Oath of Service; and receives an Enrollment Certificate bearing the great seal of the United States, and an Enrollment Badge.

He can serve his country in any one of these three separate units of the Reserve: the Agricultural Unit, the Industrial Unit, and the Vocational Training Unit. If he enters the Agricultural Unit he probably will live in a farmer's family or will work on a farm from a camp as one of a group who live together there under competent leadership and providing their own commissary; and after six weeks of six days a week or at least eight hours a day of satisfactory service is entitled to receive the Federal Badge of Honor bearing the great seal of the United States. If he enters the Industrial Unit he will work in some industry which is essential to winning the war and will gain the Federal Badge of Honor when he has rendered ten weeks of six days a week of eight hours a day of satisfactory service. The Reserve recommends that all boys who are at school remain there and that they use their spare time in vocational training for some "essential" occupation. The boy who submits himself to this training and goes into active service after training in some "war essential" occupation may enter the Reserve as a member of the Vocational Training Unit, and so is entitled, upon taking employment, to the Federal Badge of Honor.

The Federal State Director is assisted by County Directors, all commissioned by the central office in Washington. The County Director associates with himself prominent men and women of the local community. He presents the following program:

1. Enroll the boys of Reserve age in the county.

2. To provide simple and practical courses of training in the elements of farm processes.

3. To inspect the farms of farmers who desire to employ boys enrolled and to see to it that the living and working conditions upon those farms conform to standard.

4. Arrange for the supervision of boys at their work so that every boy at work in the county shall be visited by a responsible supervisor at frequent intervals and at least once a week during the working season. No group of boys so visited by any one supervisor should exceed twenty-five.

5. Arrange to organize the leisure time of boys employed, whether this employment is in groups, or whether it is in units. The organization of the leisure time of boys is positively necessary for city boys, first for their encouragement in their new and unusual surroundings, and next for the increase of their working efficiency. "All work and no play makes Jack a dull boy."

6. The enrollment of boys is accomplished by the appointing in every high school in the county one or more persons in that school to be Enrolling Officers to enroll the boys under their immediate charge into the Reserve.

C. Department of Labor, U. S. Employment Service.
Director, MR. JOHN B. DENSMORE
(Address, 1712 G Street, N. W., Wash., D. C.)

The United States Employment Service is the arm of Department of Labor through which the Government's centralized war labor supplying program is being executed. Established ten years ago, the Service was reorganized and tremendously expanded in January, 1918, to serve as the National machine for the mobilization of America's industrial army. Six months later, in June, 1918, all the production departments and boards of the Government, represented by the War Labor Policies Board, centralized in the Employment Service the recruiting and supplying of labor for war production. This was approved by the President on June 17, 1918.

The centralization program, effective August 1, 1918, as regards unskilled labor and later extended to cover skilled labor, gave to the United States Employment Service a virtual monopoly of the recruiting and distributing of labor for war production.

The Employment Service operates through more than 500 branch offices in the agricultural and industrial centers and 20,000 volunteer agents. The branch offices constitute the placing arm of the Service and the latter the recruiting arm. This recruiting service is known as the Public Service Reserve of the Employment Service and in addition to recruiting labor to be placed in war industries, including the farms, through the branch employment offices, registers engineers and other highly skilled men for Government service. The 20,000 agents cover every county and township in the country.

The Employment Service has a highly decentralized administrative system in order that the application of its program to States and communities may be flexible and adapted to local conditions. The national head is the Director General at Washington.

There are thirteen District Superintendents. Every State has a Federal Director of the United States Employment Service who is in charge of the branch offices within his State.

The office of the Director General at Washington includes a number of divisions and sections which specialize in labor supplying. Among these are the Farm Service Division, Woman's Division, Unskilled Labor Section and Skilled Labor Section. Similar specialization is had in the larger branch offices, there being in them special divisions for supplying railroad, farm, dock, mining and woman labor.

The employers and employees of the country share in the administration of the centralized war labor supplying program—from the determination of the personnel to the application of the general principles. This is done through a system of State advisory boards and community labor boards.

The State advisory boards each consist of two representatives each of the employers and employees of each State and the State director of the Employment Service, who is chairman. The community labor boards are composed of one representative each of the community's employers and employees and a representative of the Employment Service, the latter being chairman. The community boards have general charge of the recruitment and distribution of labor among local industries, utilizing the branch offices and Reserve agents of the Employment Service. The State advisory boards are courts of appeal from the decisions of the community boards and determine the application of the program to the entire State.

In keeping with the Department of Labor's policy of representative joint administration, the State advisory boards and the community boards themselves were selected by State organization committees, composed of a representative each of employers and employees and the State director of the Employment Service. In all cases, employers' and workers' representatives were chosen by employers' organizations or the State federations of labor.

The employment Service is now engaged in combing the country for unskilled workers and for machinists, toolmakers, diesinkers and other skilled craftsmen vitally needed for war production. In transferring workers from non war work to war work, care is exercised that the burden on non war industries is equalized.

The following four cardinal principles underlie the war labor recruiting program:
1. War work must have men at any cost.
2. Withdrawals of workers from non-essential industries for war industries will be equalized.
3. The volunteer principle will be followed in dealing with the individual worker.
4. Only fit men will be sent to war industries.

Following are the national administrative officers:

JOHN B. DENSMORE, Director General.

NATHAN A. SMYTH, Acting Assistant Director General and Chief of the Unskilled Labor Section.

WILLIAM E. HALL, National Director of the Public Service Reserve.

M. A. COYKENDALL, Chief of the Farm Service Division.

I. W. LITCHFIELD, Chief of the Skilled Labor Section.

MRS. MARGARETTA NEALE, Chief of the Woman's Division.

ROGER W. BABSON, Chief of the Inquiry and Education Division.

ALEXANDER D. CHIQUOINE, JR., Editor of the U. S. Employment Service Bulletin.

The district superintendents are:

District 1.—H. A. STEVENS, 807 Little Building, Boston, Mass.

District 2.—JOHN R. O'LEARY, 22 East Twenty-second Street, New York, N. Y.

District 3.—JOHN C. SAYLOR, Old Federal Building, Wilmington, Del.

District 4.—JOHN W. REYNOLDS, Cleveland, Ohio.
District 5.—RALPH IZARD, 810 East Main Street, Richmond, Va.
District 6.—CLIFF WILLIAMS, Meridian, Mass.
District 7.—P. L. PRENTIS, 116 North Dearborn Street, Chicago.
District 8.—C. C. KAVANAUGH, Little Rock, Ark.
District 9.—JAMES O'RILEY, 406 Metropolitan Life Building, Minneapolis, Minn.
District 10.—A. L. BARKMAN, Kansas City, Kan.
District 11.—H. W. Lewis, 220 Bedell Building, San Antonio, Tex.
District 12.—William T. Boyce, Claus Spreckels Building, San Francisco, Cal.
District 13.—Edgar C. Snyder, First Avenue and Union Street, Seattle, Wash.

V. COUNCIL OF NATIONAL DEFENSE
Director, MR. WALTER S. GIFFORD
(Address: Council of National Defense Bldg., Wash., D. C.)

The Council of National Defense was created by Congress in 1916 for the coordination of industries and resources for the national security and welfare, and for "the creation of relations which will render possible in time of need immediate concentration and utilization of the resources of the Nation." It is further charged with the duty of supervising and directing investigations and making recommendations to the President and the heads of executive departments as to the location of railroads with reference to the frontier of the United States, so as to render possible expeditious concentration of troops and supplies to points of defense; the coordination of military, industrial, and commercial purposes in the location of extensive highways and branch lines of railroad; the utilization of waterways; the mobilization of military and naval resources for defense; the increase of domestic production of articles and materials essential to the support of armies and of the people during the interruption of foreign commerce; the development of seagoing transportation; data as to amounts, location, method and means of production, and availability of military supplies; and the giving of information to producers and manufacturers as to the class of supplies needed by the military and other services of the Government.

The Council itself is composed of the Secretary of War, Chairman, and the Secretaries of the Navy, Interior, Agriculture, Commerce, and Labor. With the Council there acts an Advisory Commission, headed by Daniel Willard, and composed of the following members: Howard E. Coffin, Julius Rosenwald, Bernard M. Baruch, Dr. Hollis Godfrey, Samuel Gompers, and Dr. Franklin Martin.

Under both Council and Commission, many subordinate bodies of an emergency nature were created at the outbreak of the war. Of these several, notably the Committee on Raw Materials and the Committee on Supplies, have since been allocated to other departments of the Government, it being a prime function of the Council to serve as a proving ground for new phases of federal administration. The subordinate bodies of the Council are at present the State Councils Section, which organized the state councils of defense, which are in turn extended down into the communities; the Woman's Committee with its twelve thousand units over the country, the task of which is the mobilization of the woman power of America; the Highways Transport Committee, the duty of which is to utilize public highways to supplement the work of the railroads; the Medical Section and General Medical Board, with some 35 subcommittees on which are many of the leading physicians and surgeons of the country; the Committee on Labor, with various subcommittees dealing with industry and welfare questions in connection with labor; the Committee on Education; the National Research Council, acting as the department of science and research for the Council of National Defense; and the Naval Consulting Board, acting as the Council's bureau of inventions. The Council of National Defense is at this date, July 18, 1918, conducting a preliminary study of the American problems of reconstruction and readjustment at the close of the war.

Walter S. Gifford is Director of the Council and of the Advisory Commission, and Grosvenor B. Clarkson is Secretary of both bodies.

VI. UNITED STATES FOOD ADMINISTRATION
Administrator, MR. HERBERT HOOVER
(Address: 19th and D Streets, N. W., Wash., D. C.)

The United States Food Administration came into actual existence on August 10, 1917, when it was formally created by the President under the authority given him by the Food Control Act of the same date. Mr. Herbert Hoover was appointed Food Administrator by the President.

The Food Control Bill conferred upon the Food Administration powers of regulation to aid in the primary purpose of supplying our fighting forces and the Allies with food, while at the same time keeping food conditions at home in as stable equilibrium as can be attained during the cross-currents and abnormal conditions induced by war.

Thus the Food Administration's activity from its very beginning has had the double purpose of shipping the most necessary and most concentrated food overseas, and of keeping unobstructed the home channels between food producer and consumer. To assure such progress, unblocked by any sort of trade manipulation or unfair business practice which would allow any agency en route to pocket an undue profit at the final expense of the public, has been the problem confronting the Food Administration in multitudinous variations of detail.

As a means to solving food problems by those in closest contact with those problems, the Food Administration adopted a system of Federal Food Administrators in all the States and, working under them, County Administrators. This method provides a centralization of responsibility along with decentralization of actual administration; and in addition, it offers to every man, woman and child in the country the opportunity to be in closest contact with the personal representatives of the Food Administration. Indeed, it is not going too far to say that each individual in the United States has been a working unit of the Food Administration, or has at least had the opportunity to be one. This has led to the result of making families and individuals throughout the country realize their responsibility primarily toward feeding the Allies, and incidentally has quickened the public pulse in all sorts of cooperation necessary for the winning of the war.

Meanwhile, during this first year of its existence, the Food Administration sought and obtained not merely the cooperation of the public, but that of all the national food trades. Week after week and month after month since the Food Administration came into existence, representatives of different food trades and organizations have come to Washington to confer with the Food Administration. This has led to a spirit of voluntary and patriotic cooperation and to equitable regulations that have minimized the evils that inevitably result from the abnormal business situation produced by war.

Such, to treat so large an undertaking very sketchily, was the working plan under which the Food Administration has conducted its activities during the first year of its existence. It is now possible to look back and see how far it has actually justified itself by what it has contributed to the sustenance of those fighting the world's great battle against autocracy. Note, for example, the case of wheat, which has been especially needed by the Allies. Owing to the short crop of wheat in 1917 our ordinary basis of home consumption would have permitted us to send overseas less than 20,000,000 bushels. Instead of this, out of our last harvest we shipped to Allied countries about 141,000,000 bushels. This represents what was released from our own home supply by the sheer power of concerted conservation. The same encouraging results are shown in the case of meat, particularly since the transportation difficulties of last winter have been in a measure alleviated.

One could go on to quote actual statistics at great length to show tangible results of the way the public has cooperated with the Food Administration. But it will not do nowadays merely to look back congratulating oneself on past accomplishment. If the 1918 wheat crop is as large as seems to be the case, that stock must be used to form a working reserve, both in this country and in the Allied countries, to guard against such stringencies as the submarine menace has caused in the past.

Even more vital at present is the necessity for economizing and using wisely our available supply of sugar. The Allies must get their supply from us, in large measure, owing to the ship shortage which prevents sugar from being brought from Java. In addition, France has suffered from the loss of beet sugar mills in territory now occupied by Germany. In order to furnish the necessary sugar, this country must staunchly face a self-enforced ration limited enough to release what is needed for overseas shipment and still provide for absolute necessity in this country. Regulations have been formulated and put into effect, governing the amount of sugar permitted in such foodstuffs as sweet drinks and the like, but it is also necessary for the public to face its individual responsibility of cutting the use of sugar considerably below pre-war custom. France is getting but a pound and a half per person per month, when the sugar is to be had. Shall we balk at a per capita ration considerably more generous than that? Before the war England used more sugar than we. Shall we refuse to share and share alike with her now?

Six months from now will doubtless provide an answer. And the answer will be one dependent upon the character and moral stamina of our citizenry. In determining this answer the churches of this country can help the Food Administration as they have through the past year by their loyal cooperation. It is particularly well worth noting that the Catholic Church, ever since the organization of the Food Administration, has been eager in spirit and rich in accomplishment in the cause of food saving.

Speaking of organizations which represent religious faiths, Herbert Hoover wrote as long ago as October, 1917: "No other power in this country can more effectively reach the homes and put through a great systematic program of voluntary unselfish service." The truth of his assertion has been amply fulfilled. And yet, that is no reason for any relaxation of endeavor. Indeed, in a letter written to the churches of this country early this summer, Mr. Hoover says: "Our work is not yet complete. In spite of the encouraging results of our efforts, in spite of the fact that our exports of foodstuffs are constantly increasing and are approaching the minimum requirements abroad, the need for renewed devotion and effort is pressing."

That is the thought to be borne in mind and to be lived up to vigilantly and unceasingly during all the coming months. Only by such effort and devotion will it be possible to attain the goal. Yet no goal which enlists the determination and highest aspirations of the American people is unattainable.

The following suggestions for enlisting the active support of religious organizations in food production and conservation have been issued by the administration.

The daily developments in the food situation abroad and at home demanding as they do a large flexibility of program, call for the presentation to producers, dealers and consumers, of constant changes in the food regulations. This fact and the imperative need for greater production and conservation efforts, emphasize the necessity for closer cooperation between the religious organizations and the United States Food Administration.

The work that has already been done by the churches and synagogues is deeply appreciated, and the great effectiveness of this means of reaching the people is the justification for a further communication.

Where this bulletin is received by those that have already adopted the suggestions herein contained, and are closely cooperating with the Food Administrators, no change in present methods is requested. Where this cooperation has not been fully developed, however, it is hoped that this communication will lead to such development and that its recommendations will be carried out.

FOOD ADMINISTRATION ORGANIZATION.—Every State, Territory and Dependency of the United States now has a Federal Food Administration, appointed by the President. A majority of the States are being organized upon a geographical basis, with an Administrator for every county or other local subdivision.

The duties of these representatives of the Food Administration are, broadly speaking, to stimulate food production and to regulate and conserve food supplies. In the matter of production and conservation the maximum amount of intelligent publicity and cooperation is necessary. It is obvious that this may be greatly aided by the religious organizations throughout the country. Attention is particularly called to these Federal

Food organizations in each State, and it is hoped that all churches and synagogues will coordinate their activities therewith.

GENERAL PLAN.—All Federal Food Administrators (State and local) have been requested to enlist the support of all churches and synagogues located within their respective jurisdictions. The Administrator has been requested to cooperate with the State leader of each denomination in organizing within the State. Each church and synagogue, which has not yet done so, is urged to designate a food committee of one or more, to keep in close touch with the Food Administrator on the constantly developing aspects of the food situation. The committee in each church and synagogue will act as a bureau of information for the members of its organization and as a stimulus to increase activities along the conservation lines hereinafter suggested, or along any other lines that local conditions may justify.

ACTIVITIES SUGGESTED:

1. Eliminating unnecessary collations from all social functions.
2. At banquets or occasions where the serving of food is necessary, presenting conservation menus, having few courses, using local foods, and substituting other foods for those which we wish to save for export.
3. At meetings of church societies and gatherings of that nature, giving some time to consideration of food problems, as, for example:

    a. To teach conservation as a matter of self-sacrifice and to impress upon the public the first duty of feeding our soldiers and our Associates in the War.

    b. To announce and explain the constantly developing program of the Food Administration.

    c. To discuss substitutions, desirable recipes, methods of canning and drying, and the relative nutritive values of various foods.

    d. To demonstrate cooking or the use of war kitchens.

    e. To give instruction as to the most practical products to raise in home war gardens; to stimulate the raising of domestic animals, poultry, etc.

    f. To encourage consumption of local products to relieve the transportation problem. The development of home gardens and the local consumption propaganda during 1917 saved the country from great suffering.

4. Delivering frequent educational and inspirational messages from the pulpit and in the Sunday School.

5. Checking the membership to ascertain if all families are enrolled as members of the Food Administration.

6. Urging patronage of retail dealers and public eating places, which observe the Food Administration regulations.

7. Urging greater production.

VII. UNITED STATES FUEL ADMINISTRATION
Administrator, MR. HARRY A. GARFIELD
*(*Address: 18th and C Streets, N. W., Wash., D. C.*)*

The declaration of war made it imperative that more coal be produced and that all the supply that could be obtained must be rigidly conserved and equitably distributed. The Federal Trade Commission made a report on the fuel situation to Congress, which, on August 10, 1917, passed the "Lever Act." This act conferred on the President full powers, under which, on August 22 he promulgated a schedule of prices, by states for coal at the mines not under contract; and, on August 23, he appointed Harry A. Garfield, formerly of Cleveland, Ohio, and at that time President of Williams College, United States Fuel Administrator, with comprehensive power to control production and distribution of fuel and with a specific authority to fix mine prices by fields and regions in detail.

The first problem confronting the Administrator was the demand of labor to share in the increased prices of coal which prevailed as a result of the unsettled conditions. Unequal distribution, caused by competition for coal at any price, had resulted in preferential treatment and had caused embarrassment to war industries as well as hardship to domestic consumers. Conferences of mine workers and operators were held in Washington, beginning October 6, 1917, the outcome of which was a supplemental agreement to be appended to existing agreements between operators and miners. Bituminous mines were allowed an increased price of 45 cents per ton and anthracite 35 cents per ton to cover increased wages; in cases where the agreement respecting each was adopted. The operators and miners were obligated not to suspend work in case of labor disputes arising, and enforceable penalties were provided.

Mr. Garfield has surrounded himself with advisers of the widest experience in the production of coal. Cyrus Garnsey, Jr., Assistant Administrator, was formerly executive head of the Calloway Coal Company of Memphis; Director of Conservation, P. B. Noyes, formerly president of American Hardware Association; Director of Distribution, J. D. A. Morrow, secretary of National Coal Association; Director of Production, James B. Neale, operator in both the bituminous and anthracite fields of Pennsylvania; Bituminous Adviser, Rembrandt Peale, one of the most widely known men in the bituminous industry; Labor Adviser, John P. White, former President United Mine Workers of America; Transportation Adviser, G. N. Snider, coal traffic manager New York Central Lines, East; Director of Fuel Oil Division, M. L. Requa, chairman valuation committee of Independent Oil Producers' Agency of California; General Solicitor, W. T. Alden of Alden, Latham & Young of Chicago.

The large central organization in Washington has been augmented by the appointment of 48 State Administrators, acting under its direction, and they in turn are assisted by about 3,000 local or county administrators. District representatives and inspectors in each coal producing district attend to enforcement of Federal regulations. Early in 1918 a zone system of distribution was put in force to help relieve the strain on transportation resulting from war activities. A clean coal regulation minimizes the carrying of fuel not up to standard. Shipment of coal for ship bunkering is restricted to certain high grades. Priorities of shipment to industries determined by the War Industries Board to be the most essential to the prosecution of the war are enforced. Supply to industries of a less essential nature has been curtailed.

Anthracite for factory purposes has been rigidly limited and the product so restricted in its movement as to avoid any extra tax on the already over-burdened transportation systems. Increased allotments were made to New England and the Atlantic States for the year 1918—19 over the amount consumed during the year of 1917—18. Decreased allotments were made for the central and north central states and Canada, while the supply to the trans-Mississippi territory and the southern and western states was entirely cut off.

To increase production and keep the mines working to their full capacity during the summer months when they usually slow down, although transportation is easier then, a campaign urging early ordering of the year's supply was instituted by the Fuel Administration at the beginning of the new coal year in April, 1918.

A serious handicap was encountered in the calling of miners for war service. Every effort was made to keep the force remaining in the spring of 1918 supplied with orders and cars and thus eliminate any idleness.

Many methods of conserving the fuel supply have been ordered or recommended. Maximum production with minimum waste, is the program outlined by the Bureau of Conservation of the United States Fuel Administration. Every power plant in the country is undergoing inspection and is being given a classified rating in accordance with its efficiency in the use of fuel.

Saving of fuel in the operation of railway locomotives was one of the important items taken up exhaustively at the convention of the International Railway Fuel Association held in Chicago, in May, 1918, and a systematic campaign to accomplish much in this field through stoppage of leaks, cleanliness of boilers, etc., is being pushed by officials of the organizations of the railway men cooperating with the Railroad Administration. The importance of this is realized at once when it is known that the railroads consume nearly one-third of the entire bituminous production of the nation.

Figures announced by the Fuel Administration in May indicate a serious shortage for the coal year of 1918—19. The estimated requirements are 735,000,000 net tons, while the production for the calendar year 1917 was estimated at about 654,000,000 tons, which was approximately 64,000,000 tons more than in 1916 and 84,000,000 more than in 1913, these two years having been record breakers by large percentages. The country is, therefore, facing a serious shortage. Increased production over last year, if accomplished, must obtain in the face of a shortage of labor at the mines and by the further taxing of an already over-burdened transportation system. The need of extreme conservation is therefore self-evident.

Through the cooperation of the country, by the elimination of useless waste and by the careful conservation and efficient utilization of all fuel supplied, the United States Fuel Administration expects to be able to effect the distribution of a supply of coal to meet all war requirements and all necessities.

VIII. COMMITTEE ON PUBLIC INFORMATION
Chairman, MR. GEORGE CREEL
*(*Address: 10 Jackson Place, Washington, D. C.*)*

The Committee on Public Information was established by Executive order of President Wilson on April 14, 1917. Pursuant to this order it was composed of the Secretary of State, the Secretary of War and the Secretary of the Navy with Mr. George Creel as civilian chairman and executive officer. President Wilson has taken a direct personal interest in its plans and work. The headquarters of the Committee are at 10 Jackson Place, Washington, D. C., with subordinate and affiliated offices in New York and representatives in most of the associated and neutral countries of the world.

To give the greatest publicity consistent with military and naval safety, to the efforts of the American nation in the war; to drive home to all our people the aims and purposes of America and to make clear the life and death character of this struggle by revealing the purposes, methods and ideals of the war-mad nation that had imperilled our national life and even civilization itself in its lust for conquest. The Committee on Public Information has become essentially a great emergency educational institution for the maintenance of national morale behind the fighting lines. As such it serves every department of government and cooperates with every national patriotic force. An example of the latter is the League for National Unity of which Cardinal Gibbons is an honorary president.

In doing its work it has enlisted every agency of publicity and education. Pictures, posters, films, the press, cables and wireless, the schools, pamphlets, the public platform, civic, social and religious organizations have all aided either directly under the Committee or by cooperation through existing machinery. The Committee on Public Information under the direction of Mr. Creel is organized into divisions headed by a director, selected with reference to his especial qualifications for the type of work under his direction.

Ways to Help.—The Church through its clergy, schools and press has already done much toward bringing before its membership all the patriotic purposes and all the governmental needs and aims to which the Committee is striving to give the largest publicity. The field of work is still large especially among our people of foreign birth and descent, who look to the Church for leadership. The schools and universities have a great opportunity. The publications, pictures and films put out by the Committee are a great aid in the work already being done and might be more largely used. The war has brought a rare opportunity to hasten the work of patriotic education and Americanization. No other agency is more practically and potentially effective than the Church in this field.

IX. THE FEDERAL BOARD FOR VOCATIONAL EDUCATION
Chairman, HON. DAVID R. HOUSTON
(Address: Ouray Building, Washington, D. C.)

A still larger field of usefulness for Catholic Societies throughout the country is opened up by this Commission since it has for its purpose the work of reeducating men disabled in the war. During the past ten months the Federal Board has organized its staff of experts in various lines and of regional agents for inspection of all schools aided by federal funds. The Director of the Federal Board is Dr. C. A. Prosser. Under the supervision of this Federal Board war emergency training classes for conscripted men have been organized in the public school throughout the country. A series of war emergency training courses for army occupations has been prepared and these courses have been adopted extensively not only for classes organized under the direct supervision of the Board, but as well for classes organized by the War Department among men enlisted in the army and for classes conducted on a commercial basis under private civilian control.

The emergency war training bulletins of the Federal Board include emergency training courses in shipbuilding for shipyard workers, mechanical and technical training for conscripted men (Air Division, U. S. Signal Corps); training for motor truck drivers and chauffeurs; for machine shop occupations, blacksmithing, sheet-metal working, and pipe-fitting; for electricians, telephone repair men, linesmen, and cable splices; for gas engine, motor-car, and motorcycle repair men; for oxy-acetylene welders; and for airplane mechanics, engine repair men, wood workers, riggers, and sheet-metal workers.

The preparation of these courses and the organization of training classes has been undertaken at the request of, and in cooperation with the Signal Corps and the Quartermaster Corps in the War Department, and the United States Shipping Board.

Growing out of conferences between officials of the Federal Board for Vocational Education and officers of the General Staff an arrangement was perfected late in October, with the approval of the Secretary of War, for the utilization of the educational facilities of the United States by the Federal Board in cooperation with the War Department for the purpose of training drafted men in various occupations prior to their reporting at the cantonments.

Even more absorbing in its appeal to the Federal Board, because of the wide range given to vocational education as a means of insuring human welfare, has been the investigation of methods and processes developed in the belligerent countries for vocational rehabilitation of men disabled in the war. Coincidently with its organization the Board initiated its inquiries in this field, and it has pressed these inquiries continuously during the past ten months.

No other agency of the Government was prepared to enter this field, and the Government naturally turned to the Federal Board for expert service.

The enactment recently by Congress, without a dissenting vote in either house, of the Smith-Sears Act, entrusting to the Federal Board the vitally important work of reeducation and returning to civil employment men disabled in the war, is a recognition of the services of the Board during the past ten months in accumulating data relating to rehabilitation work, and in devising a scheme of organization for undertaking this work as our men return disabled from service. Here, also, it is provided that there shall be full and complete cooperation. The several Government offices concerned with the future welfare of men discharged from the army and navy, including the medical and surgical services of the War Department and the Navy Department, the Bureau of War Risk Insurance in the Treasury, and the labor exchanges in the Department of Labor, together with the Federal Board, will each render service in retraining and returning to civil employment men disabled in the war.

The Federal Board will act in an advisory capacity in providing vocational training for men during their convalescence in the military hospitals, before their discharge from the Army or Navy, and will continue such training to finality after discharge, as the civilian agency of rehabilitation and placement in industry.

X. THE AMERICAN NATIONAL RED CROSS
Chairman, MR. HENRY P. DAVISON
(Address: 17th and D Streets, Washington, D. C.)

I. RED CROSS WORK IN AMERICA AND IN EUROPE.

The American Red Cross was chartered by Congress in January 1905. It is not a Government organization; it is a voluntary aid, organization, rendering relief in times of peace as well as in times of war. It is officially recognized as such by the Government, and assists the Army and Navy whenever called upon to help care for the wounded and suffering. It is national in its scope and organization and is governed by a Central Committee of eighteen persons, among whom are representatives of the State, Treasury, War, Justice and Navy Departments. All its financial accounts are audited by the War Department and an annual report is made to Congress by the Secretary of War.

President Wilson is its President, not by the virtue of his office as President of the United States, but by election of the Central Committee. Robert W. De Forest is the Vice-President; John Skelton Williams is Treasurer; John W. Davis is Counselor and Stockton Axson is Secretary. Former President William Howard Taft is Chairman of the Central Committee and Eliot Wadsworth is Vice-Chairman. By appointment of the President of the United States there is a Red Cross War Council of which Mr. Henry P. Davison is the Chairman. The other members are Mr. Charles D. Norton, George B. Case, Cornelius N. Bliss, Jr., and John D. Ryan, up to the time he became Chairman of the Air-Craft Production Board. The Chairman and Vice-Chairman of the Central Committee are ex-officio members of this Council. Its function is to direct the work of the Red Cross in the extraordinary emergency of the war.

The work of the American Red Cross has two aspects: First, Work here in America; second, Work in Europe.

A. RED CROSS WORK IN AMERICA.

The chief phases of Red Cross work in America are:

a. Preparation for Relief Work in Europe;
b. Work among soldiers and sailors in this country;
c. Work among the Civilian Population;
d. Maintaining and Administering Funds for work at home and abroad.

a. Preparation for Relief Work in Europe, by organizing base hospitals, ambulance companies, and naval hospital units and turning them over to the War Department; by enrolling nurses and organizing them into units for service; by the mobilization and administration of volunteer effort, through the chapters and their branches and auxiliaries, for manufacturing relief supplies.

There is a very special and urgent need for nurses, and the Red Cross is appealing for them at present. Communications on the subject should be addressed to Miss Jane Delano, Director of the Department of Nursing, National Headquarters of the American Red Cross, Washington, D. C.

b. Work among soldiers and sailors in this country, which embraces a camp service that includes distribution of supplies at training camps, cantonments and naval stations, and the erection and care of convalescent houses; and the Red Cross Home Service, which keeps the men in touch with their families at home and assured of their welfare. Canteen Service is also part of the work and consists of furnishing refreshments to soldiers at railway stations when traveling. Sanitary Service, the third branch of this work, cooperates with the Public Health Authorities to safe-guard the health of the civilian population living adjacent to military zones.

c. Work among the civilian population. This work is done by the Department of Civilian Relief, which in time of peace is responsible for Red Cross relief in disasters such as floods, fires, earthquakes tornadoes and the like, and in time of war devotes its chief energy to Home Service. Home Service is that phase of Red Cross work which is concerned with the welfare in times of war of the families of men enlisted in the service of our country, and also of families, residing in this country, of men enlisted in the service of our Allies. Its object is to help keep up the morale of the men in the service by helping to maintain the morale of their families at home, keeping them in good spirits, health, comfort, and their normal standards of life.

Each Red Cross Chapter has a Civilian Relief committee as a part of which there is organized a Home Service section to look after local Home Service needs. It cooperates with all the charitable and social organizations of its community. It is composed largely of Red Cross volunteers and has a membership as representative as possible of the various local interests— church, business, professional and social work. Over three hundred thousand soldiers' and sailors' families are now enjoying Home Service, while the need for Red Cross Home Service workers is correspondingly and constantly increasing. It is one of the outstanding Red Cross opportunities for service.

d. Maintaining and administering funds for work at home and abroad. The moneys of the Red Cross are secured from membership dues and from the Red Cross War Funds raised for war relief by voluntary contributions of the people. The minimum goal set for each War Fund Campaign so far has been One Hundred Million Dollars and in each instance the amount has been over-subscribed. All expenses of the entire Red Cross organization throughout the United States are met by membership dues, and there is a handsome balance left over for disaster relief.

War relief is paid out of the Red Cross War Fund. Every dollar contributed for relief goes for war relief, and the Fund is administered by the War Council through the Red Cross organization here in America and through the Red Cross Commissions sent to various countries in Europe for military and civilian relief abroad.

B. Red Cross Work in Europe.
Red Cross work in Europe embraces:
a. Military Relief.
b. Civilian Relief.
c. Aid for Prisoners.

a. The military work of the Red Cross in Europe consists in the sending of medical and relief supplies, almost daily, from America, and their distribution in France and elsewhere; the maintaining of fully equipped rest stations for the soldiers; the operating of rolling canteens and the maintaining of stationary canteens back of the firing line; maintaining ambulance service and cooperating with the French authorities for giving medical and surgical supplies to the French Military Base Hospitals; carrying on jointly with the French Government the re-education of disabled or mutilated soldiers.

b. For the civilian population, the Red Cross is endeavoring to help keep the soldiers' homes intact; to find homes for the outcast children who have neither homes nor parents, and to help the refugees and the repatries to find a place to live until they shall be able to rebuild their homes.

c. The American Red Cross is also perfecting plans to care for Americans who may be captured and held in German prison camps. A complete scheme for sustaining American prisoners in Germany has been worked out jointly by the War and Navy Departments, and the Red Cross.

II. THE EXTENT OF THE RED CROSS.

On June 30, 1918, there were 3,855 chapters, with 14,208 branches; and in addition there are auxiliaries to chapters estimated in number to be three times that of the chapters. Any church or any group of people can form an auxiliary for the purpose of Red Cross work and give it the name of the church, or parish, or some prominent individual whom they wish so to honor. The formation of auxiliaries is one way to give local individuality to the Red Cross work and contributions.

The Red Cross has an adult membership of over twenty-one million and a Junior Membership of several million school children. The Junior Red Cross membership is the mobilization of school children and teachers into auxiliaries for Red Cross activities through the school organization, and represents an opportunity for the little ones and young children of the country to do actual work to help win the war. Any school, with the permission of its principal, may become an auxiliary, upon application to the School Committee of the Local Red Cross Chapter, and paying dues equal to twenty-five cents for each pupil, or giving a pledge of loyal service.

Nationally the Red Cross is organized into fourteen divisions, with division headquarters in thirteen large centers of the United States, and a fourteenth in Washington, D. C., in charge of the territory outside the United States. The function of National Headquarters is the determination of policy and supervision of Red Cross activities. All home activities are directed through the fourteen divisions. The work abroad is carried on by the War Council through Commissions to all the allied countries.

B. SUPPLEMENTAL AGENCIES FOR COOPERATIVE WAR WORK

I. THE YOUNG MEN'S CHRISTIAN ASSOCIATION
Chairman, MR. WILLIAM SLOANE
General Secretary, MR. JOHN R. MOTT
(Address: 347 Madison Ave., New York City.)

The work of the National War Work Council of Young Men's Christian Associations inside the camps and cantonments and at the various Army posts and Navy stations includes the erection and maintenance of the necessary service, administration, auditorium and other special buildings, and the promotion of the usual Young Men's Christian Association's program of amusement, recreational and athletic games, and social, educational and religious activities. This program is worked out in conference with the Knights of Columbus and the Jewish Welfare Board to avoid all unnecessary duplication. While the Association, as well as these organizations has its own distinctive religious affiliation, all its facilities and privileges are open alike to all men of the Army and Navy. The Young Men's Christian Association also continues the regular work, which it has conducted since 1898, at its regular army And Navy branches, which are housed in permanent buildings and provide the usual social, educational, physical and religious activities.

Overseas the Young Men's Christian Association makes similar provision for the men of the American Army and Navy, together with such additional work (*e. g.,* the operating of the post exchange) as the military authorities assign to it. It also places its usual facilities at the disposal of the French, Italian, and other Allied Armies and Navies and prisoners of war.

It has extended its work to the men in process of transit, on trains, transports, and at ports of embarkation; and to men in war industries, such as soldier loggers, men in navy yards and arsenals, and workers in shipyards and munition plants under government control.

The National War Work Council is operating in the United States alone 878 separate units with 650 buildings. There are 3,202 secretaries at work in this country, and 4,413 workers overseas, including secretaries, canteen workers, mechanics, motion picture operators, etc.

The daily attendance at the various buildings in this country alone averages over one-half million. More than thirteen million letters are written in these buildings each month.

Officers of the National War Work Council are: William Sloane, Chairman; Cleveland H. Dodge, Treasurer; John R. Mott, General Secretary; and Fletcher S. Brockman, J. S. Tichenor, Charles R. Towson and C. V. Hibbard, Associate Secretaries.

II. THE YOUNG WOMEN'S CHRISTIAN ASSOCIATION
Chairman, MRS. JAMES S. CUSHMAN
Secretary, MRS. HOWARD M. MORSE
(Address: 600 Lexington Ave., New York.)

A committee of the National Board of the Young Women's Christian Association is responsible for using the resources of that organization in helping meet the special needs of girls and women affected by the war.

The committee works

In the United States.
Establishing Club and Recreation work for girls, including a Patriotic League (for both white and colored). Providing Emergency Housing for employed girls and women. Erecting Hostess Houses in army and navy camps for women relatives and friends of the men (both white and colored). Establishing work in colored communities affected by the war. Conducting a bureau for foreign-born women, providing translations of needed bulletins, interpreters in army camps, training Polish women for reconstruction work in Poland and maintaining a home service for non-English speaking women. Providing and financing social leaders for women under the direction of the War Department Commission on Training Camp Activities. Establishing Room Registries and War Service

Centers in cities employing girls in war industries. Maintaining a Bureau of Social Morality which cooperates with the War Department in furnishing a group of women physician lecturers on social standards in war time, and also in issuing literature. Publishing a War Work Bulletin and other educational literature. Maintaining a Bureau of Volunteer Workers.

In Europe.
Providing social workers, recreation leaders, physical directors and cafeteria managers.

For American Women in France.
Nurses. Signal Corps (women). Other English-speaking women employed by the American Army.

*For French Women (*at the request of French Government*).*
Working in munitions factories. Working in stores and offices. Working in French war offices.

In Russia.
Providing leaders for club, cafeteria and educational work in three centers for Russian women.

III. THE JEWISH WELFARE BOARD
Chairman, COL. HARRY CUTLER
Secretary, MR. CHESTER J. TELLER
(National Headquarters, 149 Fifth Avenue, New York.)

Upon the entrance of the United States into the great European War, the Jews of America evinced a desire to meet the social, recreational, religious and spiritual needs of the boys of Jewish faith enlisted under the Stars and Stripes. For this purpose, a large number of national Jewish organizations, all of which are today affiliated with it as cooperating or constituent societies, organized the Jewish Welfare Board in April, 1917.

What this Board aimed to do at the outset was to help America win the war, by aiding her in all possible ways to develop a morale among her fighting men, and particularly among men of Jewish faith and ancestry. To do this efficiently and successfully, it has selected and trained a force of field workers who are sent forth to minister to the religious, social, and other needs of the boys in the various camps and cantonments of the United States.

But the Welfare Board realized that its endeavor to serve the soldiers would be only half completed by caring for their needs while in camp. In order that the men, when off duty, shall have proper facilities for wholesome recreation and pleasant diversion, it has organized local branches in towns adjacent to camps. The organization of these town branches stimulates the interest of the folks at home for the men in the service and guarantees a continuous and constructive relationship between the men and their home communities in all matters affecting their welfare. The communities aid the camp workers in the organization of their religious and recreational activities, and stimulate town hospitality, community center work, send-offs to enlisted or drafted men, hospital visitation and other personal service.

To meet the need of housing facilities for its workers, and for general welfare purposes for Jews and non-Jews alike, the Jewish Welfare Board is erecting welfare buildings. To date, it has authorized twenty-six buildings in the more important cantonments throughout the country. It provides for these buildings all necessary equipment, including books, periodicals, newspapers, stationery, etc.

With the cooperation of the Jewish Publication Society, it has published 80,000 copies of the Scripture Readings and 80,000 copies of Jewish Prayer Books and has purchased for distribution among the boys "over there," 10,000 copies of the British-Jewish Publications. It has published and distributed in cooperation with the Commission On Training Camp Activities. Yiddish translations of two sex-hygiene pamphlets, and has likewise published and distributed a Yiddish translation of a bulletin on Government Benefits.

The Jewish Welfare Board extends its services not only to men in the camps and naval stations in this country, but also to men who serve on board ships in our own waters and abroad.

IV. THE NATIONAL BOARD FOR HISTORICAL SERVICE
Chairman, DR. EVARTS B. GREENE
Secretary, MR. WALDO G. LELAND
(Address, 1133 Woodward Bldg., Washington, D. C.)

The Bureau of this important Board is 1133 Woodward Building, Washington, D. C. Address all communications to W. G. Leland, Esq.

This Board was established in May, 1917, by a group of scholars as a kind of clearing house through which the services of the historical profession might be placed at the disposal of the Government and the country. Its activities may be conveniently grouped under the following heads:

1. *Research.*—In its corporate capacity and through its individual members it has investigated various topics related to the present international crisis. The results of some of these investigations have been furnished directly to certain departments of the Government. Other material has been furnished to the periodical press, both popular and scientific.

2. *Education.*—The present situation clearly requires more than ever an intelligent public opinion regarding not only the historic institutions and ideals of the United States and the affairs of the Western Hemisphere, but also the peoples of Europe, including our enemies as well as our allies. This is essential not only in order to appreciate the conditions which compelled the United States to enter the war, but also to deal intelligently with the problems which must be solved before a just and lasting peace can be secured. In order to help teachers in presenting to their pupils and to the communities in which they live the historical background of the present crisis, numerous articles have been published through the History Teacher's Magazine, the Bureau of Education, and the Committee on

Public Information. Among these publications are a topical outline entitled, *The Study of the Great War*, and *A Critical Annotated Bibliography of the War*. So far as individual teachers have been able to work out satisfactory plans for presenting these topics to their pupils the Board will be glad to receive such information and to place it at the disposal of others who may desire advice. The Board is so ready to furnish, so far as possible, information as to competent lecturers on the war and its historical background.

3. *Cooperation with the Committee on Public Information.*—This has taken form chiefly in the preparation of a number of pamphlets, by members of the Board, in the Red, White, and Blue Series and the War Information Series. Among the numbers so prepared special attention may be called to those entitled *Conquest and Kultur and German War Practices*. Both illustrate the pains taken to secure accurate texts upon which the public may rely with confidence.

4. *War Records.*—The Board is deeply interested in the preservation of records which shall enable the future historian to present an accurate account of American participation in the war. The documents which should be so preserved include not only official records, national, state, and local, but also those of other corporate bodies such as churches, universities, the Red Cross, business corporations, etc. Even individual records such as diaries and letters may be of great importance. In this matter also the Board aims to serve as a clearing house, both giving and receiving suggestions.

V. THE TRAVELERS AID SOCIETY
President, MR. GILBERT COLGATE
Secretary, MR. ORIN C. BAKER
(Address, 465 Lexington Ave., New York City.)

Travelers Aid is a non-sectarian, non-commercial protective organization to safeguard travelers, particularly women and girls, who by reason of inexperience, ignorance, illness, infirmity, or disability, are in need of protection and assistance. Travelers Aid gives advice, information and protection to all travelers, irrespective of age, race, creed, class or sex. All services are rendered absolutely free and its agents are not permitted to accept any gratuities.

The organization had a distinct field before the war began, with workers at stations and docks in all large cities and cooperating representatives in hundreds of smaller places, and was already established and experienced when war conditions made it necessary to increase the work. Travelers Aid workers have been placed in stations in or near camp centers where before the war such work was not needed, and in other centers where the work was being actively carried on it has been intensified to meet conditions.

Travelers Aid workers meet trains and boats and offer assistance to inexperienced or unsophisticated travelers, or those who are strangers and whose friends or relatives fail to meet them. They assist those who have come to work in war industries to find employment and housing. They care for the relatives or friends of men in service until they can reach the men at the camps or on leave from the Navy.

The Aids know just where the camps are and the quickest way to reach them, and also how to find the men at the camps when their friends come without sending word in advance. They know what war work is being done by other organizations and can refer soldiers, sailors, their families or friends to proper places for lodging, for recreation, or for other needs.

The definition of Travelers Aid is so broad that sectarian, interdenominational, social, and philanthropic organizations have been able to unite for the more effective protection and assistance of travelers on humanitarian principles in the National Travelers Aid Society, which is unifying the organizations into a cooperative whole and stimulating the local work. The four points of the definition are:

First.—The investigation on request of the reasons why persons leave their home, including questionable inducements such as offers of positions, deceptive letters, addresses and acquaintances, etc.

Second.—The meeting and protection of travelers at stations and docks.

Third.—The assistance of travelers, when necessary, to suitable and respectable lodging places in the city, to trains and boats for other points, or returning them to their own homes when advisable.

Fourth.—Bringing strangers in touch with the agencies in the new community in touch with organizations that will develop them socially, mentally and religiously.

VI. THE NATIONAL AMERICAN COMMITTEE OF THE POLISH VICTIMS' RELIEF FUND

Chairman, MR. I. J. PADEREWSKI
Secretary, MR. W. O. GORSKI
(Address: 33 West 42nd Street, New York City)

The National American Committee of the Polish Victims' Relief Fund is an organization founded in New York by I. J. Paderewski, the celebrated musician, for the purpose of collecting money in the United States for the relief of Polish war victims. The offices of the organization occupy a spacious room in the Æolian Building, which the Æolian Company has kindly placed at the disposal of Mr. Paderewski free of rent. All the officers of the organization, including the present executive secretary, having spontaneously volunteered their services, are honorary members of the Polish Victims' Relief Fund; in other words, are not drawing any salaries. The New York Telephone Company has generously extended the courtesy of free local service to the Polish Victims' Relief Fund. Thanks to these propitious conditions, the National American Committee of the Polish Victims' Relief Fund has been able to bring down its expenses to the minimum figure of 1.98 per cent on the money collected; this sum representing the average of expenditures for the period from January 1, 1917, to July 1, 1917. These expenses averaged 6.60 per cent for the first period of existence of the Committee, namely, from May 7, 1915, to June 16, 1916, and they averaged 2.44 per cent for the second period, namely, from June 16, 1916, to December 31, 1916. Expenses consist of stenographers' salaries, postage, stationery, advertising, telegraph, exchange on out-of-town checks, and include the cost of transmitting the funds collected to Europe.

For the relief of Polish war refugees in Russia and Siberia money is cabled by the Polish Victims' Relief Fund to Petrograd in care of the American Embassy and is distributed among the sufferers by the Polish Central Relief Committee of Petrograd. For the relief of Polish refugees in France and Switzerland the money is cabled to local Polish relief organizations. For the relief of the populations inhabiting the parts of Poland invaded by the Germans and Austrians, all sums of money are cabled in larger amounts to the General Polish Relief Committee in Vevey, Switzerland, founded by Henry Sienkiewicz and I. J. Paderewski. This is done with the full knowledge and sanction of the state Department in Washington, D. C.

In order to avoid delay, confiscation or possible loss in transmission, the money is dispatched from Switzerland by special messengers in cash and handed to local representatives of the Committee in Poland. The messengers, who defray their own traveling expenses, are men of high standing, well-known, distinguished Poles, whose reputations are above suspicion. The local representatives in Poland are for the most part members of the Catholic Church. In their turn they distribute the funds between the most needy among the sufferers without discrimination as to creed, race, nationality or political opinion. In other words, all destitute inhabitants of Poland are helped alike, be they either Poles, Lithuanians or Ruthanians, Jews or Gentiles—all receive their share of the moderate means placed at the disposal of the Committee.

VII. THE AMERICAN COMMITTEE FOR ARMENIAN AND SYRIAN RELIEF

Chairman, MR. JAMES L. BARTON
Secretary, MR. CHARLES V. VICKERY
(Address: 1 Madison Avenue, New York City.)

The purpose of the American Committee for Armenian and Syrian Relief is to provide the necessities of life for two and a half million starving people in the Eastern War Zone; 400,000 of whom are orphan children. Relief for these sufferers is transmitted in the form of credit through the

War Trade Board and in cooperation with the State Department, thus giving assurance that the enemy or the allies of the enemy do not derive benefit from the funds given for the relief of these destitute of Western Asia.

No food is sent directly from the United States to either points within or outside the Turkish Empire. All supplies are purchased in the countries where the relief is distributed.

The American Committee for Armenian and Syrian Relief makes no distinction in race or creed. Through them the American people have sent over ten million dollars for Armenian, Syrian and Greek sufferers. These needy people are divided into the following groups: those who have succeeded in escaping from Turkey into the Russian Caucasus, those who have sought refuge in Persia, those who have escaped behind the British lines in Mesopotamia and Southern Palestine and another group who are still compelled to remain within the Turkish Empire, for it is as difficult for a Turkish subject of pro-ally sympathy to leave the Turkish Empire as it is for a Belgian to escape into France.

The work of distribution is carried on by American missionaries, physicians and teachers who have remained on the field, braving the dangers of war and pestilence to give aid to these suffering peoples. The principal relief stations of the Committee are situated at Erivan, Russian Caucasus; Teheran, Persia; Cairo, Egypt; Bagdad, Mesopotamia; Jerusalem, Palestine. Out of these larger centers radiate hundreds of smaller points.

VIII. THE GENERAL WAR-TIME COMMISSION OF THE FEDERAL COUNCIL OF THE CHURCHES OF CHRIST IN AMERICA

Chairman, ROBERT E. SPEER
Vice-Chairman, RT. REV. WILLIAM LAWRENCE
Secretary, REV. WILLIAM ADAMS BROWN
(Address: 105 East 22nd Street, New York City. Branch Office, 1112 Woodward Bldg, Washington, D. C.)

The General War-Time Commission of the Churches was created by the Federal Council of the Churches of Christ in America soon after the entrance of the United States into the War. Its purpose is to coordinate the activities of the Protestant churches, to carry on such work as can best be done in a cooperative way, and to furnish a means of united expression when such is desired.

The range of its work is indicated by the following list of some of its more important committees: Committee on Survey, Joint Committee on Chaplains, Committees on the Equipment of Chaplains, on Voluntary Chaplains, on Camp Neighborhoods, on Work in Centers of War Industry, on the Welfare of Negro Troops, on Conditions in France, on War-Time Work in the Local Church, on Social Hygiene and Sex Morality, and on Literature and Publicity.

The officers of the Commission are: Chairman, Robert E. Speer; Vice-Chairman, Rt. Rev. William Lawrence; Secretary, Rev. William Adams Brown.

The General Committee on Army and Navy Chaplains is a body cooperating with the War Department, the Navy Department and Red Cross in the selection of Protestant Chaplains. It has encouraged the formation of a Chaplain Committee, in the main Protestant denominations, and is composed of the chairmen of those denominational Committees. In cooperation with the latter it has invited many capable young ministers to enter the Chaplain Service and it has made careful investigation concerning the professional fitness of those who volunteer to enter the chaplaincy. While it is not officially connected with the War Department, Navy Department or the Red Cross, all Protestant ministers entering the Chaplaincy must have the approval of this Committee.

IX. THE BOY SCOUTS OF AMERICA
Chief Scout Executive, JAMES E. WEST
(Address: The Fifth Avenue Building, New York City.)

The Boy Scouts are trained to efficiency, self-reliance and resourcefulness, to honor, loyalty, purity and honor. Their program of recreation—education activities, endorsed by the Catholic Church and by educators of high repute everywhere, is the most effective system of boy training yet discovered. Its essential aim is good citizenship and the development of such qualities as will make for manhood of the best type.

With such a platform and such ideals, and with an enormous active membership, all pledged to practical patriotism, it is not strange that when our country entered the world war, the Boy Scouts of America were immediately in the field, ready for action, recognized by the Government and the country at large, as a significant auxiliary in the war program as well as a no less important adjunct, by way of offering a sane antidote to the evils war brings in its train, particularly the dreaded menace of increased juvenile delinquency. That service has continued from that time to this. One hundred per cent patriotism is the war time watchword of the Scout Movement, and as it numbers over 350,000 Scouts and over 90,000 Scoutmasters and Scout Officials, its influence upon the national morale can scarcely be overestimated.

Under the direct sponsorship of the Government, scouts sold 1,291,781 subscriptions amounting to $197,238,200 of bonds in the three Liberty Loan Campaigns. Up to July 31, 1918, the scouts have sold $14,930,925 worth of W. S. S. and will no doubt double the record before January 1, 1919.

Both individually and collectively, the Boy Scouts of America have loyally supported the national program of Fuel and Food Conservation and have been particularly active in the food producing end of war winning, and in spreading intensive gardening propaganda. In 1917 there were tens of thousands of scouts who had gardens themselves, or helped in those of their parents and friends. They also worked in canning factories and orchards and on farms. The same work is being done this year on an even larger scale.

All of this is being done with the cooperation of national agencies and with the personal endorsement of President Wilson, Members of the Cabinet and the various directors of wartime activities. Secretary McAdoo recently said, "The Boy Scouts of America are one of the greatest of our war facilities. They are helping us win."

Of scout service to other important patriotic agencies, it is almost impossible to speak in detail, so extensive has been the cooperation of the Boy Scout Organization with such agencies and causes. They have participated actively in all the war relief campaigns, and assisted the financial campaigns of the American Red Cross, the Knights of Columbus, the Y. M. C. A., the Salvation Army, the War Camp Community Fund, and many others of national importance at this time.

Our people are at this time anxious to give full measure of devoted service to our country in its hour of splendid stress, and we have at hand an unparalleled opportunity for mobilizing our youth for helpfulness along these lines, if we will but take advantage of it. The annual report of the Boy Scouts of America records hundreds of scout troops organized in connection with Roman Catholic Churches. There is no reason why the number should not be doubled, or trebled. On the contrary, there is every reason why it should be so doubled or trebled, not only for the sake of our boys themselves, for whom Scouting is a proven benefit, but because, by its program and methods already worked out and practicable and successful to a remarkable degree, the Movement offers a channel for patriotic activities on the part of our Catholic youth.

It may not be here amiss to remind our people that the Scout Movement has the unqualified approval of his eminence John Cardinal Farley and other prominent leaders of our faith, that it is widely accepted by the Roman Catholic Church both here and in Europe, and that there is an authorized Roman Catholic Bureau for extension of Scout Work. Victor F. Ridder of New York is the National Scout Commissioner for Scout Work in Roman Catholic Churches.

Anyone interested in securing information as to the character of the Movement, the procedure involved in starting scout troops in Catholic Churches, and ways by which Scouting can be utilized for practical service along patriotic lines, should address communications to the Boy Scouts of America, National Headquarters, 200 Fifth Avenue, New York City.

X. THE NATIONAL ORGANIZATION FOR PUBLIC HEALTH NURSING, WAR PROGRAM COMMITTEE
615 19th Street, N. W., Washington, D. C.

"One of the greatest forces in protecting the health of the Nation is the public health nurse," says Newton D. Baker, Secretary of War.

The object of all public health nursing is the prevention of disease and the reduction of infant mortality through the instruction of the individual in the home. This instruction may be given by the visiting nurse who cares for the sick mother or child, staying long enough to give expert nursing care, and to carry out the orders of the physician; by the infant welfare nurse who teaches mothers how to care for themselves and their babies so that instead of one baby out of every ten dying before the age of one year as happens in the United States, we have more lusty children who will grow to strong maturity; by the school nurse who in her turn follows up the medical inspectors' diagnoses and convinces parents of the necessity of correcting physical defects, such as the draft has shown to have been neglected in the past; by the hospital social service nurse who links the hospital with the home thus ensuring the cure that preventible bad home conditions might have retarded or even made impossible; by the tuberculosis nurse who teaches her patient those lessons of isolation and disinfection which protect his family and the community; by the industrial nurse who is able to get in close contact with both employer and employee, making a good understanding between the two, and making factory conditions more healthful with the result of fewer absences and a smaller labor turnover.

France and Italy, recognizing their need of the expert knowledge that alone can adequately meet the need of their people, are turning to their new ally for public health nurses to establish tuberculosis and infant welfare stations, and the Red Cross is sending them the most experienced women available.

Our own Government has called upon the public health nurses to assume the health problems of the Extra-Cantonment Zones, and the associate secretary of the National Organization has been released to the

Federal Public Health Service as inspector in these zones. To her has been delegated the problem of correlating all public health nurses in these zones, and to submit plans of organization so that there may be no duplication of effort and so that the zone may be made safe for our soldiers.

Every one wants to help the Children's Bureau in its splendid program to save 100,000 babies between April 6th, 1918, and April 6, 1919. The best way to do this is to insure the part this program which involves the placing of a public health nurse in every community not already so provided.

In 1917 the war so increased the interest of the country in conserving the health of the people and in consequence so increased the demand for public health nurses, that it was necessary for the National Organization for Public Health Nursing to start an active campaign to increase the number of such specially trained women.

To lay the foundation stones of such a campaign the Organization joined most heartily with the other national bodies in the recruiting for the training schools for nurses, as among the young women now entering the training schools are the public health nurses of the future.

But the need is immediate, and every effort is being made urging nurses, who have never before specialized in public health work to take one of the many courses in theory and practical work to different parts of the country in order to fit themselves for responsible work. The Educational Secretary has arranged also for emergency training courses of ten weeks in several states.

www.ingramcontent.com/pod-product-compliance
Lightning Source LLC
Chambersburg PA
CBHW050440010526
44118CB00013B/1614